Robert P. Green, Jr.

The Study and Teaching of Economics

Roman F. Warmke
Ohio University

Raymond H. Muessig
The Ohio State University

Steve L. Miller
The Ohio State University

Charles E. Merrill Publishing Company
A Bell & Howell Company
Columbus   Toronto   London   Sydney

The Study and Teaching of Social Science Series
Raymond H. Muessig, Editor

Published by Charles E. Merrill Publishing Co.
A Bell & Howell Company
Columbus, Ohio 43216

This book was set in Souvenir
Cover Design Coordination: Will Chenoweth
Production Coordination: Linda Hillis Bayma

Credits: Specific acknowledgments of permissions to use materials appear on page vi, which is to be considered an extension of this copyright page. Standard credit and source information appears in the *Notes*.

Photos: Cover by Gene Gilliom; Rohn Engh, 3, 56, 92, 95; The Firestone Tire and Rubber Corp., 5; Ohio Bureau of Employment Services, 13. Loan application form on page 105 courtesy of Railroad Savings and Loan Company, Columbus, Ohio.

Copyright © 1980 by Bell & Howell Company. All rights reserved. No part of this book may be reproduced in any form, electronic or mechanical, including photocopy, recording, or any information storage and retrieval system, without permission in writing from the publisher.

Library of Congress Catalog Card Number: 79-90845

International Standard Book Number: 0-675-08166-1

1 2 3 4 5 6 7 8 9 10—85 84 83 82 81 80

Printed in the United States of America

Foreword

The Study and Teaching of Social Science Series is composed of six books, *The Study and Teaching of Anthropology, The Study and Teaching of Economics, The Study and Teaching of Geography, The Study and Teaching of History, The Study and Teaching of Political Science,* and *The Study and Teaching of Sociology.* In the larger part of every one of the six volumes, the social scientist was asked to deal with the nature and development of his field, goals of and purposes served by the discipline, tools and procedures employed by scholars, significant and helpful literature in the field, and fundamental questions asked and ideas generated by the academic area. Writers were challenged not only to provide solid subject matter but also to treat content in a clear, concise, interesting, useful manner.

Each of the six works in the series concludes with a chapter entitled "Suggested Methods for Teachers," which was written after reading and considering the complete manuscript by the individual social scientist.

In a number of ways, *The Study and Teaching of Social Science Series* resembles *The Social Science Seminar Series* (published in 1965) from which it is descended. The idea for *The Social Science Seminar Series* came to me in 1963, when the structure-of-the-disciplines approach in social studies education was receiving considerable attention in publications, meetings, and projects. At that time, social studies educators and supervisors and others were searching for substantive material concerned with the essence of academic disciplines and for down-to-earth ideas for specific classroom learning activities. They sought materials which would spell out and facilitate ways of translating abstract social science concepts and generalizations into concrete inquiry strategies that would be meaningful and appealing to children and youth. In the early sixties, some historians, economists, sociologists, anthropologists, political scientists, and geographers were trying to think of ways that others could teach respectable social science to elementary and secondary students about whom the academicians had little knowledge and with whom university scholars had no experience. And certain classroom teachers and others in professional education were informed with respect to human growth and development, child and adolescent psychology, theories of instruction in general and of social studies education in particular, day-to-day classroom organization and management, etcetera, and could work and relate well with younger pupils. These practitioners, however, readily admitted their lack of the kind of breadth and depth in all of the various social sciences necessary to do even an adequate job of defining and interpreting the disciplines. They frequently added that they had insufficient financial resources, time, energy, background in methods and media, creativity, and writing talent to produce for themselves and others the pages of requisite, appropriate, fresh, variegated, pedagogical alternatives needed to reach heterogeneous collections of learners at all instructional levels.

Thus, it seemed to me that a very real need could be met by a series of solid, practical, readable books where the content on each discipline would be written by a specialist in that social science and where the material on teaching strategies would be developed by a specialist in social studies education.

Now, some brief comments are appropriate regarding the revised and many completely new approaches for the last chapters in *The Study and Teaching of Social Science Series*.

The 1965 *Social Science Seminar Series* was designed primarily to assist K-12 teachers in the application of a structure-of-the-disciplines social studies theory in their classrooms. Since the needs and pursuits of the many users of the series have changed and become more diverse than they were in 1965, and since I, too, have changed in the ensuing years, this 1980 rendering is considerably more eclectic than its progenitor. Rarely is there a one-to-one relationship between a specific teaching method and a particular, overall theory of social studies education. Additionally, a myriad of instructional media may be matched with different philosophies and techniques. And, a single theory of social studies education need not be followed by an entire school district, by a whole school, by all of the teachers at the same grade level, or even by a given teacher throughout a school year with each of the students. The suggested methods in the last chapters of *The Study and Teaching of Social Science Series*, then, can be used as presented, modified to suit various classroom situations, adapted to complement different social studies theories, and altered to fit numerous goals and objectives. In the final analysis, a key test of a teaching method is the extent to which it touches the life of an individual learner in a meaningful way.

A Special Acknowledgment

When Charles E. Merrill Publishing Company expressed an interest in my plan to develop a series of texts in social science and invited me to submit a detailed proposal, I immediately asked Dr. Vincent R. Rogers (then at the University of Minnesota and now at the University of Connecticut) if he would join me as co-editor of the series and co-author of the chapters on instructional approaches. I worked with Professor Rogers on the refined plan that was sent to and approved by Merrill. Vin Rogers and I had written together previously in an easy, relaxed, compatible, mutually advantageous manner. We were both former classroom teachers who had become university professors of social studies education. We shared a feeling for the needs, interests, problems, and aspirations of students and teachers, had a serious commitment to the social sciences, and were familiar with a variety of instructional media. But, more than any other person I could find and attract as a co-worker on the endeavor, Rogers could translate significant ideas into functional, sequential, additive, meaningful, imaginative, enjoyable methods. Vin did his share throughout the entire undertaking, and he was responsible for the securing of all but one of the initial social science authors of the first version of this program. Our writing together on *The Social Science Seminar Series* went swimmingly, and we emerged even better friends than before.

When Merrill requested that Dr. Rogers and I revise and create new material for our concluding chapters for the six books in *The Study and Teaching of Social Science Series,* I anticipated the pleasure of a collaboration again. However, Professor Rogers already had too many previous commitments to undertake something as time consuming and demanding as this effort, and he had to withdraw, unfortunately. True to his generous personal and professional nature, Professor Rogers told me to use any or all of the ideas he and I had developed separately and together about fifteen years ago. We blended so well in the sixties, and so many things have happened since that time, that I doubt whether I could easily distinguish between our original suggestions anyway. Thus, my sincere thanks to Vin for his contribution to the first series and to this second undertaking.

Raymond H. Muessig

Acknowledgments

From SIDEWALK STORY by Sharon Bell Mathis. Copyright © 1971 by Viking Press, Inc. Reprinted by permission of Viking Press, Inc.
Reprinted with permission of Macmillan Publishing Co., Inc. from THE BAD TIMES OF IRMA BAUMLEIN by Carol Ryrie Brink. Copyright © 1972 by Carol Ryrie Brink.
From JUST THE BEGINNING by Betty Miles. Copyright © 1976 by Alfred A. Knopf, Inc. Reprinted by permission of Alfred A. Knopf, Inc.
From MR. AND MRS. BO JO JONES by Ann Head. Copyright © 1967 by G. P. Putnam's Sons. Reprinted by permission of G. P. Putnam's.
From SURPRISE FOR MRS. BURNS by Glennette Turner. Copyright © 1971 by Albert Whitman & Co. Reprinted by permission of Glennette Turner.
Excerpts abridged from pp. 50-52 "I brought you... to decide what he would like...." in HENRY HUGGINS by Beverly Cleary. Copyright 1950 by William Morrow and Company, Inc. By permission of the publishers.
From HEY, BIG SPENDER by Frank Bonham. Copyright © 1972 by Frank Bonham. Reprinted by permission of the publishers, E. P. Dutton.
From NO PROMISES IN THE WIND by Irene Hunt. Copyright 1970 by Charles Scribner's & Sons. Reprinted by permission of Charles Scribner's & Sons.
"Laid Off" by Holly Near. © Hereford Music 1973. © Redwood Records 1976. All rights reserved. Reprinted with permission.
Words and music for "Village Ghetto Land" by Stevie Wonder and Shatema Byrd. Copyright © 1976 by Jobete Music Co., Inc. and Black Bull, Inc., Hollywood, California. Used by permission.
"Show Biz Kids." Words and music by Walter Becker and Donald Fagen. © Copyright 1973 by MCA Music, a Division of MCA, Inc. New York, New York. Used by permission. All rights reserved.
"Burn Down The Mission," Lyrics by Elton John and Bernie Taupin. Copyright © 1970 Dick James Music, Ltd. All rights for the United States and Canada controlled by Dick James Music, Inc., 119 West 57th Street, New York, N.Y. 10019. International Copyright Secured. Made in U.S.A. All Rights Reserved.
"Imagine." Lyrics by John Lennon. Copyright © 1971 by Northern Songs, Ltd. All rights reserved for the U.S.A., Mexico, and the Philippines controlled by Maclen Music, Inc. Used by permission. All rights reserved.

Preface

This book was written primarily for three audiences: students preparing to become teachers, teachers, and interested persons who want a basic understanding of how our economic system works.

Most persons who are about to read a book like to know why the book was written and what suggestions the author has to make the reading more enjoyable and effective.

First, this book was prepared because there was a definite need for it. Most beginning economic textbooks are written with the implied assumption that the reader will continue the study of economics and become a professional economist. A common tendency of writers of economics textbooks is to make the treatment of the subject matter extremely "rigorous" and, as Thomas Carlyle once noted, "dismal." The author of this book views economics as exciting, dynamic, relevant, and extremely useful for learning how to use and participate in the economic institutions of society and for functioning more effectively as a consumer, producer (worker), and a citizen-voter.

Economics is concerned with subject matter that touches the lives of all of us. If one is to understand the great debates that go on in the world around us, a knowledge of economics is essential. A basic assumption of this book is that everyone needs a fundamental understanding of how the economy operates. The second assumption is that most readers of the book will not go on to become professional economists.

A feature of this book with which you should be aware is that it follows a definite "pattern of learning" theory. The content unfolds logically and systematically. Each chapter builds on the material presented in previous chapters. The author suggests that the most beneficial and effective way to read the material presented is to follow the sequence of the chapters as presented. In the first chapter, for example, you are introduced to the vocabulary of economics. Each subject matter has its own terminology. You must master this terminology before you can move to the next step. Once the vocabulary is mastered, you are introduced to the "kit of tools" used by economists. The methodology used by economists is then pursued in subsequent chapters to analyze the economic system.

When you have mastered the contents of this book, you should be able to function relatively well as your own economist. Economics is an applied science. This point of view does not underestimate the necessity of knowing background economic theory. A skilled surgeon must, for example, be well versed in physiology. However, a knowledge of physiology is not sufficient if the surgeon is unable to apply this knowledge under practical conditions. The same reasoning is true with economics. You must have a background knowledge of economic theory if you are to apply this knowledge in meeting everyday economic situations and to function effectively as a producer, consumer, and citizen-voter.

The material presented in this book is a result of the author's approximately thirty years' experience working with teachers. Consequently, the material has been thoroughly read and criticized by students, experienced teachers, economists, and others who are familiar with economic teaching, theory, and practice. To these persons, the author wishes to extend grateful appreciation. In the final stage of publication, the text was thoroughly reviewed by Raymond Muessig and Steven Miller, both of The Ohio State University.

To you, the reader. May your study of economics be both enjoyable and worthwhile.

Roman F. Warmke

Contents

one	**What Economics Is All About**	1
two	**Economic Problems, Goals and Policies**	9
three	**A Model for Analyzing an Economic System**	21
four	**Circular Flow Analysis**	36 *some criticism*
five	**The Households: Personal Economics**	50
six	**Business Firms**	60
seven	**Government: Spending and Taxing**	74 *"Starts well then gets harder to understand."*
eight	**International Trade**	82 *last section somewhat conf.*
nine	**Money and Credit**	91
ten	**Financial Institutions**	100 *One of best.*
eleven	**Money and Monetary Policy**	110
twelve	**Suggested Methods for Teachers**	123
	Index	153

one

What Economics Is All About

Probably one of the first phrases you learned as a child was "I want." If you are like most people, there are many goods and services that you would like to have that are beyond your means. Also, you have certain *needs* such as food, clothing, and shelter to stay alive and live reasonably well. Therefore, you have to make choices to determine which goods and services you will buy and which you will not. A nation is also faced with making choices since it too cannot have all the goods and services that its citizens would like to have. Your wants and needs, like those of a society, must be satisfied through mental and physical efforts. *Economics is basically a study of the choice-making process used by individuals and total societies in their attempt to satisfy their needs and wants for goods and services.*

In this chapter you will find the answers to these questions:

1. How does economic scarcity lead to the making of choices?
2. What is the real cost of satisfying our needs and wants?
3. What are the basic economic questions that every society must answer?
4. What is a traditional economy?
5. What is a market economy?
6. What is a directed economy?
7. Why are most economies called "mixed economies?"
8. What are the important characteristics of the United States economy?

Scarcity, Choice, and Allocation

Stated simply, *economics* is a study of the process by which people make and spend their income. You can also think of it as a study of how people satisfy their wants and needs for goods and services. Even more specifically, economics is a study of the *process* by which people attempt to get the most satisfaction possible when they cannot buy all the goods and services they would like. This process is sometimes called *economizing*. An *economy* is the economic system of a country or an area. For example, we speak of the economy of the United States, the French economy, or the Russian economy. If you refer to the French economy, you are referring to the total of all economic activities in France.

In some rare instances, it is possible for a person to be able to enjoy all the economic goods and services that he or she wants or needs. This is an unusual situation. Most individuals, as well as *all* nations, must economize. When a person's or a nation's wants are greater than the resources available to fulfill them, we say that economic *scarcity* exists.

Scarcity and Choices

An *economic good* is any material object that is scarce enough that someone is willing to pay money for it. Stated another way, a good is scarce when there is not enough of that type of good to satisfy all human wants for it. Almost any item that you own would qualify as an economic good. The book that you are reading is an economic good. So is your ballpoint pen and the breakfast you had this morning. Economic goods are not free.

An *economic service* is any personal service for which someone is willing to pay money. The services of a domestic worker or a doctor serve as examples. Unlike economic goods, economic services cannot be stored and used later. They are available only at one time.

Economic goods are classified as either *consumer goods* or *capital goods* (also called "producer goods"). The term *consumer* refers to the ultimate or final user of a good. Consumer goods and services are those purchased by the *final user*. Capital goods (or producer goods) are used in the production of other goods. A printing press used to publish a newspaper would be an example of a capital good. The purpose of using the printing press is to produce another product—namely newspapers. All types of tools, machinery, equipment, industrial buildings, farms, and raw materials with which you are familiar are examples of capital goods.

Some goods are so abundant that they are available without paying money for them. For example, you do not pay money for the air you breathe or for drinking water that flows from a natural spring. A *free good* is one that has no monetary price attached to it. A free good is not scarce. If there is a cost involved in purifying the air you breathe or tapping the water you drink, these goods cease to be free goods and become economic goods. You will note that it is much easier to think of examples of economic goods than it is to think of examples of free goods. Free goods are, of course, very important to us, but they are not a part of the study of economics.

An *economic want* is the desire for an economic good or service. Your desire to see a particular movie for which you are willing to purchase a ticket is an example of an economic want. Most of us have other wants that are extremely important to us but are not in the category of economic wants. For example, we have a desire for love and affection from our family, respect and admiration from our friends and acquaintances, recognition for our accomplishments, and freedom from worry and anxiety. These wants are extremely important, but they are not a part of the study of economics unless *there is a monetary value* (or price) attached to them in some way. For example, if a person has difficulty adjusting to his or her role in life and seeks the advice of a psychiatrist in order to reduce worry and anxiety, an economic want comes into existence since there is need for a monetary payment.

Our economic wants are many and varied, and choices have to be made.

Since human wants are greater than the goods and services available to fulfill them, goods and services must be distributed or allocated. Therefore, resources such as land, labor, and capital (called *factors of production*) used to produce goods and services need to be allocated. The process is called *resource allocation*. Both individuals and societies are faced with the problem of resource allocation.

Assume, for example, that you have only three dollars available to you at a given time. Assume that a price of a movie ticket is three dollars and the price of one of your favorite foods is also three dollars. You cannot have both your favorite food and go to the movie. If you decide on the food, its *real cost,* or *opportunity cost,* is the movie. The opportunity cost (or real cost) is the value of that which you give up by making your decision. The cost of a used automobile, for example, may be a vacation foregone. For a businessperson the cost of a delivery truck might well be some tools and machinery that would be useful to the business.

Nations, as well as individuals, are faced with the need to make choices. Choices made by a nation also involve opportunity costs. To achieve certain goals means foregoing others. A country at war, for instance, makes a choice to produce military equipment at the sacrifice of roads, schools, and other types of production.

Basic Economic Questions

Every nation, no matter how well developed, is faced with answering the following four basic economic questions:

1. WHAT goods and services should be produced?
2. HOW should the goods and services be produced?
3. HOW MUCH should be produced?
4. FOR WHOM should the goods and services be produced?

The study of economics involves an analysis of the WHAT, HOW, HOW MUCH, FOR WHOM questions. These questions are examined briefly in the following sections.

Coordination of an Economic System

Economies can be classified as (1) traditional, (2) directed, (3) market, or (4) mixed.

Traditional Economies

In a traditional economy, economic life is determined by such things as custom, habit, and religious traditions. The basic economic questions are answered based upon past patterns. For example, in a traditional economy, the same agricultural fields tend to be used for the same crops year after year. Or a certain crop rotation plan might have been passed down from generation to generation. The basic rule is to follow the same approach that has been used in the past.

In a traditional economy, an individual tends to rely on the group for his or her survival and for the admiration and social standing that he or she desires. Very frequently, religion and magic serve as forces that motivate the individual.

An individual's share of the production is determined by his or her social or political status. The status of a family is also passed down from generation to generation.

In a traditional economy there are few savings and as a result only a small amount of money is channeled into capital formation. The growth rate, therefore, in a traditional economy is extremely low and results mainly from customs that have been established through time.

Directed Economies

Under a *directed economy,* the basic economic decisions are made by a central authority, which may consist of either a person or a group. The wishes of the central authority are imposed upon the members of the total society by some method of political force.

The members of the directed society are dependent upon the central authority for their sustenance and, therefore, accept the allocation decisions made. The central authority decides how much of the total resources will be set aside for the future. In this way, the central authority decides the amount of goods that will be used for capital formation to promote the future growth of the economy. In like manner, the central authority decides the current rate of production of consumer goods as well as the composition of that production. The pattern of income distribution is usually designed to conform to the particular plan established by the central authority.

Market Economies

In a market economy, most production decisions are made by the owners of the business firms. Sometimes these decisions are modified through collective action as expressed through the government. For your analysis at this point, however, assume that the business firms are free to make production decisions without government intervention.

Generally businesses will produce those goods and services for which they can receive the greatest profit. For our purposes, the term *profit* is defined as the amount of money remaining after all expenses of production are paid. The expenses of production must also include a salary for the owners of the business if they manage the business enterprise. Quite often, people fail to take into account the total cost of doing business when they are determining profit. One must be careful to include all costs so that an accurate statement of the profit of the business firm is determined. For example, owners of businesses would receive salaries if they worked for other business firms. Costs of this type are called *implied costs*. They are implied in the sense that the business firm does not actually have an outlay of money for these costs, but they are real indeed. Another example of an implied cost would be the interest that a businessperson could receive for use of his or her money if the money were deposited or invested elsewhere rather than in a person's own business. Thus, the prospects of making a profit will determine whether a particular good or service is produced. The prospects of making a profit in a business will, in turn, depend on whether consumers express a demand for the goods or services of the business firm.

In order to obtain the greatest profit possible, the owner or manager of a business will attempt to produce goods in the most efficient manner. The owner has to combine the total resources in such a way that he or she will produce the greatest quantity of goods and services at the lowest cost.

Normally individuals operating a business will attempt to employ the *principle of specialization* to increase production. The principle of specialization refers to assigning one person to the performance of a particular task rather than to have one person complete an entire process. For example, in the assembly of automobiles, one worker might be assigned the task of assembling a wheel as the car moves along the

Many businesses employ the principle of specialization to increase production.

assembly line. Other workers are assigned similar specialized tasks. No worker is responsible for the entire assembly of the automobile. Rather, the specialized tasks are combined to complete the total operation. In this fashion it is usually possible to assemble an automobile with greater speed and efficiency than it would be if one person completed the entire operation.

Specialization is also sometimes called *division of labor*. Specialization, or division of labor, that leads to greater production is sometimes called *economies of scale*. When production is increased, more money is available for labor. In addition, the owner or manager of the business is able to generate higher profits.

Some generally recognized advantages of specialization include:

1. An increase in production,
2. The development of greater skills,
3. A savings in time,
4. Lower production costs,
5. The employment of some people who might not otherwise be employable,
6. The continuous and economic use of tools and equipment,
7. A spirit of interdependence.

Some of the generally recognized disadvantages of specialization include:

1. Dependency of one worker upon another,
2. Work that is sometimes monotonous,
3. A decrease in the pride of workmanship,
4. A decrease in total job ability since a worker becomes highly specialized at a specific task,
5. Difficulty for a worker finding employment if a particular skill created through specialization is no longer needed by a business firm.

An economy attempts to produce all that it is capable of producing by having all resources of the economy totally employed and operating at maximum efficiency. Unfortunately, this goal is never completely obtainable. All economies experience some unemployment or have some people who are not working up to their full capacity.

The question of how much to produce involves a decision of how much should be consumed now and how much should be put aside to improve the production capacity in the future. For example, if all the goods and services produced were consumed, there would be no resources remaining to be used to produce tools and equipment, which increase the production capacity of a nation. The only way that a nation can grow and improve its production capacity is to improve its stock of capital goods. Thus, the opportunity cost of greater production in the future is often less consumption at present.

In a market economy, the distribution of goods and services is determined by the amount of money consumers have available to spend—either individually or collectively through government. Most people must work and earn an income so that they can buy the goods and services that they need and want. Some people may have sufficient income and wealth through inheritance or other sources so that they can work solely for the enjoyment and satisfaction they get from their efforts. If, however, you are like most of us, that is not your particular situation.

Your ability to purchase goods and services depends upon both your wealth and your income. Your *wealth* is the total value of all those things that you own at a given time; it is your stock of goods. *Income* refers to the money you receive as a result of your production efforts in a certain period of time; it is a flow of wealth over a period of time. Services cannot be part of wealth because they cannot be accumulated. You may, for example, be able to increase your wealth by saving money from your income and investing it in activities that also earn money for you. The wealth of a nation, or public wealth, consists of public goods or those owned by a government. Private wealth consists of goods owned by individuals.

People usually receive income in proportion to their contribution to the production process. A person whose skills are more in demand will generally receive a higher income than one who is unskilled. For example, a doctor can expect to enjoy a higher income than an unskilled laborer. A person who has a very unusual skill is also frequently rewarded a relatively high income even if the development of the skill took little effort on his or her part. For example, an attractive movie star with natural acting ability might receive a relatively high income even though her or his attractiveness is basically a gift of nature. In economics, such monetary return is called an *unearned increment*. Most of us do not, however, possess these unique attributes and we must compete for our incomes by making a contribution to the production process. One of the best ways to achieve a higher income is to become more productive. Generally, if you improve your skills through education or special training, you will also increase your earning capacity.

Mixed Economies

Actually, there probably are no pure economic systems. A market economy will tend to have elements of the directed economy as well. Even in a market economy, certain collective decisions are made by the government that direct the course of economic activity. For example, price controls have been used from time to time in the United States. Likewise, an economy that is basically a directed form will apply elements of the market system to determine resource allocation. For example, the Soviet Union rewards plant managers on the basis of goods sold rather than simply on the amount of goods produced. Every system has some elements of the traditional, market, and directed systems. Thus, all systems tend to be *mixed systems*. We use the designation of traditional, directed, and market merely to label the main characteristics of a system.

Characteristics of the United States Economy

An understanding of some economic characteristics of the U.S. economy will help you to analyze how the economic system is coordinated. By understanding the characteristics you will gain insight into the resource allocation process. You will also understand the nature of the flow of goods and services and the flow of money. Some economic characteristics that are important in the U.S. economy include (1) private property, (2) the market system, (3) profit motivation, and (4) competition.

Private Property

In the United States, private individuals have the right to own and use property for their individual pursuits. As an income earner, you must, of course, pay your local, state, and federal taxes. Once these obligations are met you are able to keep as much of your income as you wish. The portion of your income that you keep, whether it be in cash or other forms of material assets, is known as *private property* (your wealth).

Your tax money is frequently used to buy *public property* consisting of such items as public buildings, schools, parks, and other facilities provided by the local, state, or federal government.

The Market System

The U.S. economy tends to be market oriented. In fact, many of the collective decisions made by the government are designed to make the system more market oriented in the long run. For example, the government will frequently assist local businesses through loans and other incentives so that they will be able to operate on their own more efficiently in the future.

Profit Motivation

Another characteristic of the U.S. economy is that it tends to be motivated by profit incentives. People are encouraged to pursue business activities that will lead to a profit. There is a general acceptance of the notion that people will work harder if they are able to derive personal gain from their efforts. Consequently, the production activities are motivated through profits rather than by control, punishment, or fear.

Competition

Another basic characteristic of the U.S. economy is its reliance upon competition to produce more and better goods and services. *Competition* is the effort of many business firms or individuals acting independently to attract customers. Business firms compete with one another by offering customers better products, lower prices, and better services than they are able to receive from other firms. Competition forces business firms to be constantly on the look-out for more efficient practices so that they can offer better products and services at lower prices.

In the United States several federal laws have been passed to assure competition. Ruthless business practices are regulated by the federal government so that in the long run businesses can compete on a more favorable basis.

In some areas of economic activity, it is not desirable to have competition. For example, it is inefficient to have competing water lines, electricity, and mass transportation systems. These are areas that are called *natural monopolies*. A monopoly exists when there is only one seller of a good or service. In the United States, natural monopolies are tightly regulated.

This chapter provided a basic understanding of economics. In the next chapter we will examine economic problems, goals, and realities.

two

Economic Problems, Goals and Policies

As you already know from chapter 1, the basic economic problem is a result of human wants being greater than the resources available to fulfill them. Consequently, individuals as well as nations must economize. They must establish priorities for their wants and make their choices accordingly.

Choices must be made within the environment that exists. All societies—even the most developed—face certain problems that tend to retard economic development. At other times, economic development can be used to temper some of the problems of society. To fully appreciate and understand the role of economic policy—particularly the political policy used by government—you must be alert to certain types of problems of society that exist in most nations. Once the problems of society have been identified, then basic economic goals can be examined in relationship to these problems. The interaction of basic economic goals and problems of society gives rise to public policies.

In this chapter you will find the answers to these questions:

1. What are some of the basic problems of society faced by developing and advanced economies?
2. What are the basic economic goals of most economies?
3. What role does economics play in public policy?

Problems in Developing and Advanced Economies

No nation has developed its productive capacity to the maximum extent ossible. In this sense, all nations are in some stage of development. Nonetheless, there is great discrepancy in the distribution of income among the nations of the world. The poorest half of the world receives only 8 percent of the total world income. By contrast, the United States, with only 6 percent of the world's population, receives one-third of the world's total income. Western Europe, with 10 percent of the world's population, receives 25 percent of the world's income. Even in the United States, which enjoys a relatively high per capita income, pockets of poverty do exist that retard economic development.

Poverty and Economic Underdevelopment

The elimination of poverty is not only a civilized undertaking; it also makes excellent economic sense. People living in poverty add little to the economic development of a nation.

When the per capita income for an entire nation is relatively low, there are generally some underlying reasons that must be examined before it is possible to undertake courses of action to eliminate poverty. An understanding of the basic causes of world poverty will help you to understand the major conditions that stand in the way of economic progress in many countries throughout the world.

Low Agricultural Productivity. Most poor countries are predominantly agricultural. However, not all agricultural countries are poor. Australia, Denmark, and New Zealand serve as examples of agricultural countries that enjoy relatively high per capita income. Thus, you must remember that it is not the agricultural emphasis that makes a country poor; it is, rather, low agricultural productivity—low output per worker in agriculture.

Low agricultural productivity results from (1) farming small plots of land, (2) using primitive agricultural methods and tools, and (3) employing a system of absentee ownership. Low agricultural productivity almost always exists in a trad tional economy. Plots of land have often been divided through inheritance. The methods and tools used do not change from generation to generation. Local peasants who farm the land for a city dweller or absentee landlord lack incentive since they know only too well that little of the return will be shared with them. City dwellers, in turn, have little incentive to make improvements on the land since they frequently hold the land primarily for social prestige or economic security.

Fragmentation of the Economy. *Fragmentation* of an economy exists when there is no national market. High mountain ranges or wide rivers without bridges might divide a country into small sections. Such conditions make it difficult to develop a national market. Unfortunately, however, many countries that face topographical problems of this nature are too poor to develop the transportation systems necessary to correct the situation. In order for the private economy to develop, public funds must be spent for certain types of *social overhead capital.* Examples of social overhead capital include expenditure to provide adequate transport, communication, utilities, education and training, health and family planning, and other social and community services. The money invested in providing such services is called social overhead since the cost and the benefits are spread socially rather than privately. Still, these facilities must be provided before it is possible to develop a national market.

Lack of Adequate Financial Institutions. Many countries with a low per capita income have inadequate financial institutions. As you know from chapter 1, an economy is able to grow only through improving its capital formation. Some institutions that facilitate the process of saving and lending are commercial banks, savings and loan institutions, insurance companies, and credit unions. When the financial institutions are not available to supply the credit for improving the capital base, economic growth is retarded.

Lack of Technical Skills and Education. Economic growth as well as poverty are closely related to the level of technical skills and education that exist in a given nation. Many economists estimate that as much as 20 to 25 percent of the total growth of a nation is related to the technical skills and education of the population.

In countries that are extremely poor, the educational systems are often weak. The reason for this is simply that a poor country is unable to supply the funds needed for good education. Good education, in turn, is needed to raise the country from its depth of poverty. The result is *a vicious circle of poverty,* as illustrated in figure 2-1.

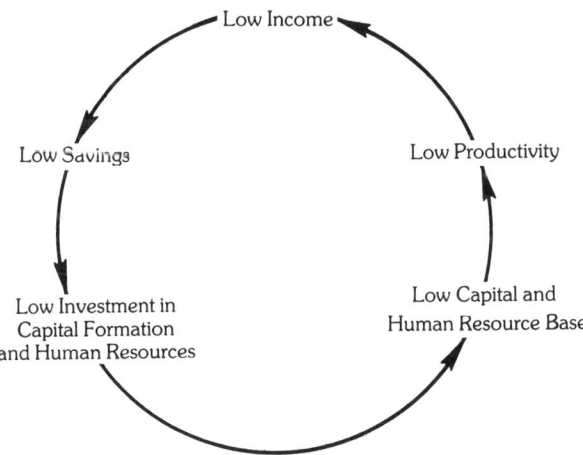

Figure 2-1. *The vicious circle of poverty.*

Administrative Difficulties. Countries with low per capita incomes must rely heavily upon economic planning. In the lesser developed countries, private business investment is seldom adequate to promote the desired growth rate since these investments must come from savings. In a country where the level of living is low, there is a tendency for incomes to be spent on the consumption of goods and services and for savings to be low. Consequently, in order to enjoy a higher growth rate, economic planning becomes necessary as a tool of government policy.

Economic planning, in turn, calls for high-level technical and administrative skills. In many countries, it is difficult to find competent people to fill the civil service positions that are necessary to carry out the administrative plans. Sometimes government positions are awarded through favoritism rather than according to the ability of the person employed. Another problem that is even more acute is that a competent civil servant frequently receives a salary which is much less than he or she could earn in private business. Remember that the type of civil service position that we are considering demands a high level of technical and administrative skill. Private industry tends to put a premium on such abilities and will frequently offer substantially higher salaries than those offered by the government. As a result, many able civil servants tend to leave public service to join private firms. A rapid turnover of people in positions of major responsibility tends to lead to inconsistency and inefficiency in the implementation of plans.

Population Explosion

Closely linked with the problems of poverty is the problem of population explosion. In order to experience real economic growth, the income of a nation must rise at a rate more rapid than the rate of its population increase. For example, if a nation's income were to increase by 8 percent and the population were to increase by 10 percent, then the average income per person would be less after the change in income and population than before these changes occurred. Developing nations generally experience difficulty in maintaining a rapid growth rate due to the lack of capital formation. Ironically, it is in these same countries that the population growth rate tends to be extremely high. Many experts believe that the per capita income in many underdeveloped countries actually declined in recent years. Most governments today encourage the development of family planning associations as a part of their general policy to increase the real income of the people. Only insofar as the rate of increase in the number of people is less than the rate of increase in the production of goods and services will there be an increase in the real per capita income.

Discrimination

Most nations experience some form of racial, religious, sex, age, or other type of *discrimination*. At times the discrimination is subtle, but, nonetheless, it exists. A caste system is an example of discrimination. Sometimes, discrimination is more a result of economic tradition than it is of outright discrimination. For example, in the United States more women hold secretarial positions than men. Racial and other forms of discrimination are an economic waste. People who are not allowed to achieve their full potential do not make the contributions to society that would be possible without discrimination.

Unemployment and Underemployment

A high rate of *unemployment* means that not all resources available are being used productively. High rates of unemployment are more common in the lesser developed countries than in the developed countries. Often the labor force (people able and willing to work) is not as mobile, and the level of training of the labor force does not match the job opportunities that exist.

Sometimes a person might be employed in a position that does not take full advantage of his or her skills and training. Such a condition is called either *underem-*

Economic Problems, Goals and Policies 13

When supply exceeds demand, unemployment increases.

ployment or disguised unemployment. Underemployment has essentially the same effects on an economy as unemployment. If it were possible in an economy to have all people employed and each person working at full capacity, the economic growth rate would be enhanced. However, unemployment and underemployment are often the consequences of economic underdevelopment. In recent years some of the more developed nations have also experienced recurring conditions of chronic unemployment. No matter how well developd an economy is, if the quantity of goods and services available exceeds the quantity demanded, there will be a tendency for unemployment and underemployment to exist.

Inflation

The purchasing power of money declines during a period of *inflation* and tends to penalize individuals who save their money and those who are on fixed incomes.

Suppose, for example, that you are able to save $1,000 and that you put it in a bank to earn 5 percent interest a year. If the inflation rate that year were 10 percent, the purchasing power of your $1,000 would actually be only $900 at the end of the year. Even if you add your interest income of $50, you still have purchasing power of only $950. On the other hand, if you had borrowed $1,000 at 9 percent interest for the year, you would have to pay back—in real purchasing power—less money than you were given at the time the loan was made.

People on fixed incomes experience a real decline in their purchasing power during a period of inflation. Often those who can afford it least suffer most during a period of inflation. Inflation has been described as "the most unfair tax of all."

There are basically three types of inflation: (1) *demand-pull,* (2) *cost-push* and (3) *administered pricing.* Demand-pull inflation exists when the demand for goods and services exceeds the supply of goods and services available and thereby pulls prices up. Cost-push inflation exists when the cost of producing goods increases and pushes prices up. The increased prices are passed along to the consumer when cost-push inflation exists. Administered pricing exists when business firms are in a position to actually fix the prices of goods and services and tend to establish prices at an increasingly higher rate without the corresponding increase in production. An example of administered pricing would be the increase in the price of oil established by Oil Producing Export Countries (OPEC) in the 1970s. Methods of controlling or reducing inflation are discussed in chapters 7 and 11.

Malfunctions in the Market Mechanism

Even highly developed countries experience frequent malfunctions in the market mechanism. In less developed nations, the lack of competition is frequently even more pronounced. A market condition exists in certain rural areas of Malaysia that has been called the *"M-M" system.* The M-M system refers to a condition where one person or business firm has gained so much economic control that he or she has become basically the only seller—therefore a monopolist—and at the same time the only buyer—called a monopsonist—of the goods and services produced by the people in a given region. Even when the conditions are not as extreme as the M-M effect suggests, collusion among producers is common in fragmented local markets. A person's chances of economic success in a fragmented market are more a matter of political and family connections than of ability or efficiency.

The lack of mobility of the labor force also creates malfunctions in the market mechanism. Population increases in the rural sectors frequently force members of the agricultural community to seek jobs in urban centers. These individuals are generally not trained to cope with the industrial jobs and living conditions in the city.

Pollution

In recent years, people have become increasingly concerned about the environment. Now when people talk about economic growth, they frequently add the question, "Growth for what?" If growth pollutes the air we breathe or the water we drink, we can well question the desirability of such growth.

Essentially pollution is a cost of production that has not been paid as a part of the production process. Pollutants dumped into rivers and streams that kill off the fish and other forms of marine life involve a real cost. If we do not clean up the rivers and streams, we shall have to forego the products destroyed as a result of pollution. The cost of controlling pollution can be placed on (1) producers, (2) consumers, (3) the general public through action by the government, or (4) a combination of any or all these groups.

Controlling Big Business, Big Labor, and Big Government

If a country wishes to maintain an economic balance, it must regulate the activities of big business and big labor. Certain businesses can develop into monopolies with enough economic power to charge prices higher than would be possible under intense competition. In a like manner, huge labor organizations are sometimes able to create disruptive economic disturbances. All countries employ certain restrictions upon big business and big labor to regulate certain aspects of their behavior. There is a further concern, however, that excessive regulations not lead to disruptive big government.

Uneven Distribution of Wealth and Economic Opportunities

Even in countries where the total national income is high, many people are frequently poor because of an uneven distribution of wealth. Governments attempt to correct imbalance through their taxing and spending policies.

Controlling Crime

A society pays for the cost of crime (1) in crime prevention programs, (2) by loss to individuals and businesses through theft, sabotage, etc., (3) by maintaining penal and correction institutions, (4) by loss of income foregone by individuals who are confined, and (5) for rehabilitation programs when an individual has been returned to society after a period of confinement.

Where crime is widely prevalent, it tends to discourage many forms of business activity and thus hampers economic development. In addition to the economic realities of crime, its existence lowers the quality of life of a society.

Maintaining National Security

In many respects, the economics of maintaining national security is similar to the economics of crime. In many countries today—if not most—the greatest public expenditure is for national defense. Frequently the national defense budget is about half of the total national budget.

Much of the money spent on national defense does create certain jobs and, therefore, generates income for those employed. These people could, however, be employed in more productive capacities if the need for national defense were not present. For example, the building of an irrigation dam will do much to enhance the future economic development of a nation. By contrast, the development of a bomb is designed more to destroy resources than to develop them. The opportunity cost of the bomb might well be a dam that is not built. Consequently, a stable international environment that would reduce the need for defense expenditures would do much to enhance economic growth.

At this point, you have probably become impressed with the fact that activities that make sense for humanitarian reasons often make good economic sense as well. The costs of poverty, discrimination, unemployment and underemployment, crime and war are high indeed. In a sense, they represent "luxuries" that countries can ill afford if they are to enhance economic growth and improve the quality of life.

Basic Economic Goals

In some economies, the productive resources are owned and directed by government. They are owned by the group (all citizens combined) and not by individuals. The leaders set the goals. Thousands of decisions must be made by the leaders, and they may be right or wrong. Great power is in the hands of a few who decide how resources will be used to fulfill wants and how each person will share in production. In most "free" or "market" economies, millions of people decide their goals. Through elected officials or representatives, decisions are made as to the goals that will be directed by the government. Individuals, however, are free to use their labor, their savings, and other resources to satisfy their own wants and the wants of others. National goals, as a result of choices, are political decisions, but the decisions are made through democratic political processes.

In market-oriented economies, people individually and as a group must set their goals and make their choices based upon careful reasoning. No nation can have everything it wants. The society cannot have all the personal pleasures, leisure, security, food and clothing, good highways, police protection, and government controls without making choices. For instance, citizens of a nation must decide how much freedom they are willing to lose if decisions are made for them by the government.

How much of your income are you willing to give up for a government service? Should the government spend money to strengthen the military or should the government spend it on our schools? Should we as citizens spend millions of dollars to have four-lane highways or should we spend more for health and welfare? Shall we spend billions of dollars for guns and missiles or more for public housing? These are some of the many basic questions that we must face as consumers and citizens.

We have through the years established certain national economic goals upon which most people agree. People in most countries generally agree that a nation should strive for economic (1) freedom, (2) efficiency, (3) growth, (4) stability, (5) justice, and (6) security. Not all countries give the same priority to these goals, as you will see later. Also, several goals often conflict with one another.

Economic Freedom

Economic freedom refers to an individual's freedom to make economic choices. Each person is free to make choices but must decide what he or she wants and set a goal. For instance, people must choose their mode of earning a living or choose between different ways in which they could spend their income. As indicated previously, the real or opportunity cost of any choice is what people must give up to gain what they want. A person might, for example, have to decide whether to spend money for a vacation or for more education, to buy a pair of shoes or other clothing if the person cannot buy both, to make a down payment for a house or to buy a new car, or whether to save or to spend. If people are to make wise decisions, they must think carefully about the value of each choice. Since economic freedom is basically a personal matter, we shall discuss it in more detail in chapter 5 where we will analyze personal economic goals.

Economic Efficiency

Economic efficiency refers to making the most efficient use of limited resources. Most goods and services have multiple uses. Land, for example, can be used to produce wheat or corn or can be used for pasture for beef cattle. Farmers attempt to determine what use of the land would net them the greatest return. More than that, they try to determine the right amount of lime and fertilizer to use, the crop rotation schedule, and other conservation practices that will provide them with the greatest net profit. That combination of resources that brings about the best or optimal level of production is considered to be the most efficient economic mix.

Economic efficiency can be viewed from the point of view of the individual consumer, the producer, the government, or the total economy. The pursuit of economic efficiency by the different individuals or groups might result in a conflict. For example, farmers might find an economic mix that will improve their efficiency to the point that a farm surplus will be created for the total economy. Similarly, a producer might, through a vigorous marketing campaign, increase his or her share of the market at the expense of another producer. The businessperson who gains through this procedure has found an economic mix that is efficient for that person. However, the cost of the marketing campaign might be inefficient when viewed from the point of the total economy. Conflicts in goals are commonplace. In the examples given above, conflicts that arise within a particular goal, namely economic efficiency, have been examined. In the presentation that follows, conflicts between and among goals will be discussed.

Economic Growth

Economic growth refers to an ever-increasing level of living. Most people expect to be better off than their parents and to have more goods and services for enjoyment. As we have increased our technology, our capital supply (tools and better equipment), and our education, we have been able to produce more and better goods and services per person. In general, we accept the notion that we will continue to improve our level of living through economic growth. Further, if we are to minimize poverty and unemployment, then we need to pursue economic growth as a desirable objective.

Economic Stability

In any economy there are likely to be fluctuations in economic activity. *Economic stability* refers to smoothing out the ups and downs of business activities. Stability exists when there is a high level of employment without inflation or deflation. Under inflation, money loses much of its purchasing power, and inflation is, therefore, particularly hard on individuals whose incomes are relatively fixed—for example, retired people. Severe deflation, such as that experienced in the 1930s could be equally undesirable in that it brings about mass unemployment, human misery, and a waste of economic resources. When there are serious fluctuations in the economy, efforts tend to be concentrated on speculation rather than production. For instance, when prices rise sharply, some firms hold back goods from the market because they expect prices to rise further, causing shortages for other firms. Most people want neither inflation nor deflation; they want economic stability.

Economic Justice

Economic justice refers to the distribution of wealth. As indicated previously, wealth is the total money value of the things we own at a given time. We should keep in mind that wealth is made up of tangible goods that have a money value because they are relatively scarce, useful, and people want them. Income is a person's reward for his or her share in producing goods and/or services. Income can come from wages, interest, rent, profits, or transfer payments. A transfer payment is an exchange of payments between two or more people that creates no additional total income; one now has more money, the other less. With the exception of transfer payments, income may be viewed as the reward for performing economic services.

Most of us as individuals want more wealth—we want to own more land, buildings, stocks in companies, and personal possessions such as automobiles and good clothes. Income enables us to get these things. Income, however, is our return for having produced. Therefore, how do we become more wealthy? Some people inherit wealth. More commonly, however, we become more wealthy by working, producing, saving, and investing.

Economic Security

Economic security refers to the desire to have every person maintain a certain minimum level of living. Examples of programs designed to create economic security include care for the aged (such as medical insurance programs), the unavoidably unemployed (such as unemployment insurance and government training programs), the dislocated worker, aid for depressed areas, and some form of farm program (such as price supports). These programs will be treated in more detail in later chapters. Not all people agree on the types of economic security that should be provided, but nearly everyone supports some form of economic security.

Public Policies: Choices Must Be Made

Economics is a way of thinking. You can use economic analysis to improve your day-to-day participation in the economy. Governments use economic analysis to improve the level of life* for their respective societies. Therefore, it is appropriate that we started this chapter with a discussion of some of the major problems faced by most societies. The economic goals of a country generally indicate deeper and broader objectives that involve both economic and noneconomic ramifications. Thus, when we speak of economic growth, we generally have as our major objective a better level of living for more people. Economic growth is one way to achieve this broader objective. It is also a way to reduce poverty.

Note that there is an interaction between the *problems of society* and the economic goals. The desire of the society to eliminate all forms of discrimination generally is accompanied by a modification in the income distribution pattern of the nation. Consequently, this objective of the society is closely related to the economic goal of justice. A society's objective to control inflation is very much related to the goal of stability. Thus, wherever feasible, appropriate economic goals are given an order of priority to solve certain problems of society.

---

*Level of living refers to the actual quantity of goods and services available in a society. This stockpile of goods and services can be measured and priced. *Standard of living* refers to a goal or way of life desired; it is the quality of living. A knowledge of art or music cannot, for example, be measured and priced, but such knowledge increases a person's standard of living.

Economic Problems, Goals and Policies

The priority that a society gives to solving certain problems affects the economic goals directly. For instance, if a society places a high priority upon eliminating unemployment and underemployment, the programs pursued could be inflationary. In this case, the economic goals of justice and security have higher priority than the economic goal of stability.

The very way in which a society defines its major problems brings about a redefinition of economic goals. For example, if a society passes minimum wage legislation, it has redefined what is meant by economic justice. Similarly, if a government takes control of a business enterprise that was formerly operated by the private sector, a redefinition of economic freedom occurs. Economic goals are used primarily to achieve broader aims or objectives. Consequently, there is continuous interaction between economic goals and the problems of society. Thus, economics is a social science that is vitally related to the problems of society.

The Use of Public Policy

Figure 2-2 illustrates how *public policy* results from the interaction between the problems of society and its economic goals.

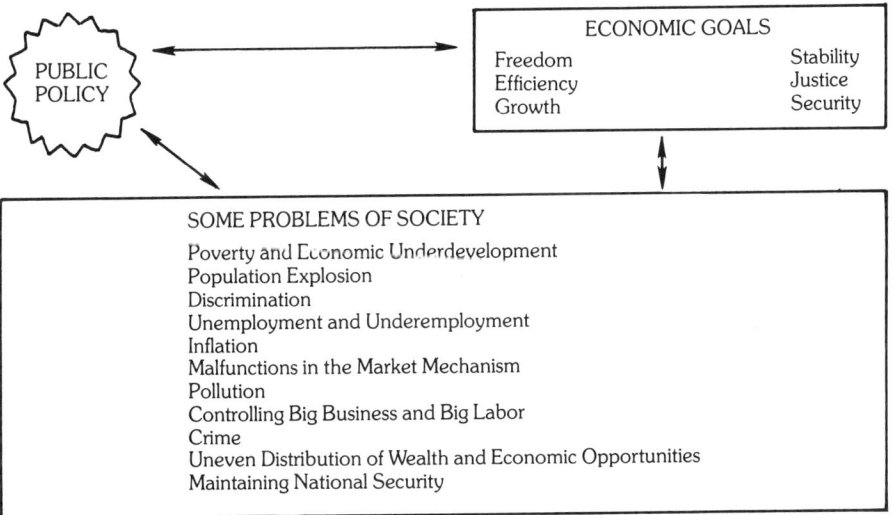

Figure 2-2. *Public policy results from the interaction between the problems of society and its economic goals.*

Sometimes public policy is used directly to achieve an objective of society. Even when this direct approach is used, the effect will be reflected in one or more of the economic goals. For instance, if a society takes direct action to control crime, economic justice, efficiency, and security will be affected. Quite possibly, certain of the other economic goals would also be affected. There is a conflict among the economic goals as well as among the objectives of a society.

Sometimes a public policy will come about directly from the economic goals themselves. For instance, a society might well accept the notion that economic growth is feasible without considering directly the broader objective of overcoming poverty. More likely, however, the broader objective of eradicating poverty will also be in the background, and the focus is simply on the economic growth because it is a straightforward and direct tool for achieving the objective.

To further analyze economic problems, goals, and policies, a model is useful. The descriptive model introduced in this chapter is completed in the following chapter.

three

A Model for Analyzing an Economic System

The central purpose of this chapter is to provide you with a tool or aid (model) for your further study of economics. A model is a representation of reality. There are several types of models. For example, there is a descriptive model. A photograph of the Taj Mahal might, for instance, be used to describe the beauty and symmetry of that magnificent structure. The photograph is, of course, not the Taj Mahal. However, it is useful for describing it. It is a *descriptive model*.

Sometimes a *predictive model* is useful. A dress pattern serves as an example. The pattern is, of course, not the dress. The pattern is two-dimensional. The completed dress is, however, three-dimensional. Nonetheless the dress pattern takes into consideration certain elements that are useful to predict how the dress will fit. Once the initial work on the dress has been completed, the dress will be tried on to see how it fits. Generally, certain adjustments will have to be made. The model seldom predicts with complete accuracy. Usually it must be altered several times. Consequently, there is a constant movement back and forth from the model world to the real world.

A *conceptual model* is a special kind of model. The word *conceptual* refers to "of the mind." A conceptual model, then, is a model created by the mind. There is no way to go to the real world to check if a conceptual model actually exists. The mathematical model used in such precise maneuvers as launching a space vehicle is an example that exists in reality; still, such models are indispensable for certain predictions.

A Model for Analyzing an Economic System

The model that you will examine in this chapter is essentially descriptive. It will provide you with an overview of the study of economics. In a way, the model might be viewed as a map. In this case it is a general map of economics. In a like manner, if you were going to take a trip across country in the United States by automobile you would probably start by looking at a map of the entire country. However, once you are on your journey, if you are lost in a particular town, you would undoubtedly look at a detailed map of that town. In the discussion that follows, we will look at the total picture of economics. In subsequent chapters, we will examine the parts in more detail.

In this chapter, you will find the answers to the following questions:

1. What is the Gross National Product (GNP)?
2. What are the basic components of the GNP?
3. How does the market mechanism function?
4. When and how is public policy used to influence economic activity?

The Gross National Product and Its Composition

The *Gross National Product (GNP)* is used to measure the total output of an entire economy for a given period of time (usually a year). It is called "gross" since it measures all the goods and services produced. It is called "national" because it includes the goods and services for the entire nation. It is called "product" because it is a measure of the production of goods and services. The GNP is simply a shorthand way of expressing the total monetary value of all goods and services produced in a given nation over a given period of time.

You must be cautious in determining GNP to be certain that no times are counted more than once. That is why you must count only the final dollar value of each good or service. For example, when a consumer buys a pair of rubber boots, the purchase price includes the cost of the latex (raw rubber from the tree), processing latex to sheet rubber, and other materials and services needed to provide the consumer with the final product—rubber boots. If you added the value of latex, sheet rubber, and the rubber boots, you would have counted the first two items more than once. Chart 3–1 helps to make this clear.

Chart 3–1

Stages of Production	Value Added	Total Value
Rubber producer produces latex	$1.00	$1.00
Rubber processor turns the latex into sheet rubber	$1.00	$2.00
Boot-maker uses the rubber to make boots	$1.50	$3.50
Boot wholesaler sells to boot retailer	$2.50	$6.00
Retailer sells boots to consumer	$1.50	$7.50
TOTAL VALUE	$7.50	$7.50

A Model for Analyzing an Economic System

Thus, the final value of the good is the same as the total of the *value added* at each stage. You can simply use the final selling price of goods or services to calculate GNP or you can use the value added.

There are four basic buyers of goods and services: consumers (C), business firms or investors (I), government (G), and foreign buyers (F). Note that F represents exports minus imports; it is a net figure. The formula for referring to the combined purchases of these buyers is

$$GNP = C + I + G + F$$

Final goods may be either consumer goods or capital goods. The former is designated by the letter C — purchases by consumers. The latter goods are purchased by business and we use the letter I to designate these purchases. The letter I represents business *investments* in tools and equipment, buildings, and inventories which are not sold to the final customer. Business firms buy many things from one another to be used in the process of production. Only when business firms sell their products to final customers do these products become a part of C. You should note that for purposes of national income accounting, new residential housing is also considered to be a part of I rather than a part of C. That is, real estate owners "invest" in residential housing and then "rent" the houses, perhaps even to themselves. Such a procedure provides a clean way of accounting for an otherwise mixed and possibly confusing consumer-business expenditure in our economy.

The same precautions that must be taken into consideration when analyzing the expenditures of business firms must be noted when dealing with foreign purchases. If GNP is to measure the dollar value of all goods and services produced *within* a country in a given period of time, the imports must be subtracted from the exports. Therefore, it is possible for F to be either a positive or negative figure. If exports exceed imports, the figure will be positive, and vice versa.

GNP Is a Flow

When we say that the GNP of the United States is, for instance, two trillion dollars, this does not mean that we could go out and add up the market value of all goods and services in the United States and come up with the total of two trillion dollars. What it means is that the United States is producing at a rate of two trillion dollars a year. Consequently, the GNP is a measure of the *rate* of production. Probably a way to remember this point is to think of all production taking place in such a way that all goods and services (or price tags for services if you wish) could be placed on a conveyor belt that would carry these goods and services to an open field where they would be stored for a period of one year. Now if we were to enter that field after one full year of production, we would, in fact, be able to add up the prices of goods and services to determine the GNP. The point, however, is that goods and services are constantly being used and are not stored up over a period of time. GNP is a measure of the flow of goods and services produced. It tells us the rate of production.

Some Limitations of GNP as a Unit of Measurement

Indispensable as GNP is in economic analysis, it does have certain limitations with which you should be familiar. Basically there are four:

1. *The Gross National Product is counted in money terms, not in physical units.* As a result, the GNP will not tell you how many goods and services were produced; it simply gives you the market value. Consequently, if prices are higher in one year than another, the GNP will be higher even if the actual volume of output is unchanged or lower.

Economists "correct" the GNP for price changes so that output can be compared from year to year. The procedure for making this correction is simple, and later on in the text the method will be presented to you. At this point, however, it is important for you to note that when we speak of the "real" GNP we are merely referring to GNP figures that have been corrected for price changes over the years.

2. *The GNP does not reflect all changes in the quality of output.* The second limitation of the GNP is that it does not measure the quality of a good or a service. For example, the GNP may not take into account all the improvements that have been made in automobiles over the years. It merely reflects the present price of automobiles. Or, children's toys may cost more but not be made as well. GNP merely reflects price, not quality.

3. *The GNP does not reflect the purpose of production.* Another limitation of GNP is that it measures simply the quantity of life and not the quality of life. Money spent for drug abuse or for military weapons is given the same consideration in GNP analysis as money spent for improved health care or for the construction of an irrigation dam. Consequently, the GNP does not tell us whether or not we are "better off" from year to year. It is simply a measure of our level of output.

4. *The GNP includes only goods and services that are for sale.* Probably the most outstanding example of goods and services that are produced but do not become a part of the GNP are the services of spouses (usually wives) in maintaining their households. If, however, we employ a cook or a maid or a babysitter, the money spent for these services does become a part of the GNP. Other examples of production not included in the GNP include fine poetry or works of art created but not offered for sale or a brilliant manuscript that is never published.

As you can see, the GNP is an approximation of the total output of the nation. In fact, many interesting and somewhat amusing possibilities for increasing or decreasing the GNP exist. For instance, the GNP will decline if a man marries his cook. This is true even if he provides her with an allowance as great or larger than she received as a salary when she served as his cook since allowances are not counted in the GNP figures. Another interesting example arises if we assume a situation where two families each do their own laundry. The GNP would rise if these two families would exchange their laundries and pay each other an identical sum for laundry services. If neighbors mow each others lawns during vacations, the GNP is not changed. If they pay each other's sons or daughters to mow lawns while they are absent, the GNP is increased.

The GNP, indispensable as it is, is only an approximation of the true value of the total output. Some economists have suggested subtracting from the GNP costs of pollution and the like. The resulting figure would undoubtedly be a better measure of "real" total output, but such procedures for determining GNP are not used widely.

At this point, one important question you might ask is: What are the limitations to the total amount of goods and services that a given country can produce? Obviously, there are some countries that are richer than others—where the GNP in proportion to the population is higher. A country's ability to produce goods and services depends upon a number of factors such as the quality and quantity of land, the availability of skilled labor, natural resources, including climate and geographical location, level of technology, political and administrative efficiency, and entrepreneurial skill. An understanding of what a country can produce can be obtained by looking at the concept of *production possibility*.

Production Possibilities

To gain an understanding of production possibilities, assume a simple economy that has only two possible kinds of output: corn or wheat. If all the land, labor, and capital were used to produce corn, the total production would be 1,000 bushels of corn a year. If, however, the total of all available land, labor, and capital were used to grow wheat, the total production would be 600 bushels of wheat a year. These two extremes, then, illustrate the production possibilities in our imaginary economy.

Chances are, however, that we would like to have both corn and wheat. The various combinations that might be possible are shown in figure 3–1, which is called a *production-possibility curve*.

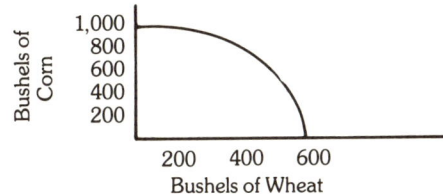

Figure 3–1. *Production-possibility curve.*

Over time it is possible for the production-possibility curve to expand in two ways:
1. The quality and quantity of available resources (factors of production) may change.
2. The technology available may change.

Suppose, for example, that it becomes commonplace in our imaginary economy to harvest two crops of wheat every year. This production possibility is illustrated in figure 3–2. Under this arrangement, combinations can be found along the curve that permit increased production of both wheat and corn.

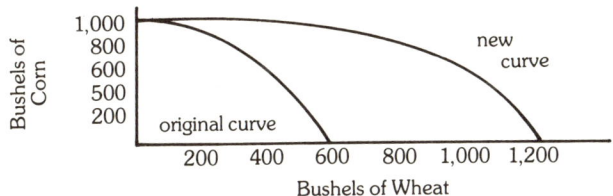

Figure 3–2. *An increase in the production of wheat.*

As another example, assume that technological advances—the use of fertilizers and improved farming techniques—increase the production of corn as well. This causes a shift in production-possibility curve, as illustrated in figure 3–3. Under this combination, even greater production possibilities are possible for both products.

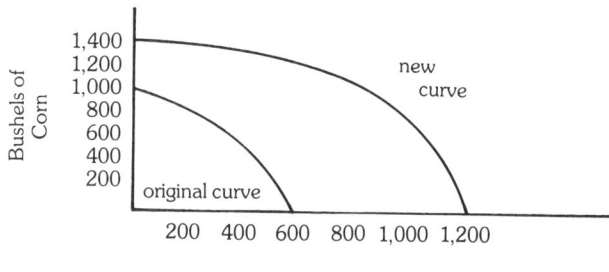

Figure 3-3. *Production of both corn and wheat.*

The production-possibility curve shows the output possibilities *when all resources are in use*. When some of the resources are idle, the actual combinations of output fall to the left of the production-possibility curve. Point F, for example, in figure 3-4 represents a production point where some resources are idle. Illustrated in figure 3-4 is the principle of increasing costs or the law of increasing costs. Note the shape of the

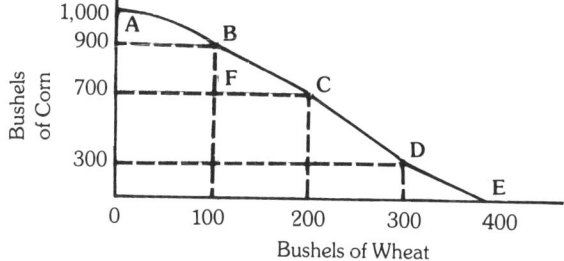

Figure 3-4. *A production—possibility curve.*

production-possibility curve; it is concave to the origin. To obtain additional quantities of one of the commodities, say wheat, ever-increasing quantities of the alternative commodity, corn, must be sacrificed. Suppose this hypothetical economy is now located at point A on the production-possibility curve. It is using its entire resource base to produce corn; it is at the same time producing no wheat. If 100 bushels of wheat are produced (point B), the cost of the 100 bushels of wheat will be the 100 bushels of corn not produced. If the economy wants to produce a second 100 bushels of wheat (point C), the cost will be 200 bushels of corn not produced. In moving from point C to point D, the cost of the additional 100 bushels of wheat will be 300 bushels of corn not produced. Finally, in moving from point D to point E another 100 bushels of wheat will have been obtained at a cost of 400 bushels of corn given up. As resources were shifted from corn to wheat production, each additional increment of 100 bushels of wheat cost more in terms of the quantity of corn given up. The reason for this phenomenon of increasing cost is that as resources are shifted from one line of production, corn, to another line of production, wheat, resources most suitable for production of corn (land, labor, and capital that are relatively productive in corn) are shifted to wheat procedures where they are less productive with the consequent increase in corn given up to obtain added units of wheat. The same increasing-cost phenomenon can be observed when the resource base is shifted from wheat production to corn production.

The production-possibility curve shows a number of things. For instance, it illustrates the concept of opportunity cost. The cost of more wheat is a reduction in production of corn. The cost of having more corn is in turn the reduction in the production of wheat.

The curve also illustrates the economic concept of scarcity. Note that it is not possible to produce any combination of corn or wheat that would fall to the right of the curve. The curve illustrates that a country must make production choices. If we use figure 3–4 as our production-possibility curve, in no instance can our example country produce more than one thousand bushels of corn or four hundred bushels of wheat.

Interaction of Supply and Demand: The Market Mechanism

The second component of our model is an analysis of how supply and demand interact in the market to create prices. We have, in the course of our discussion of GNP, used the term *prices,* and we also talked about cost, both in terms of opportunity cost and money cost. We also noted that we use prices of goods and services produced when we want to obtain total GNP. What determines the price at which a particular good will sell? This is the same as asking what determines how much of a particular good will be produced in the economy. Economists use demand-supply analysis to answer the above question, and we shall now look at the main outlines of this analysis.

The Market

For this part of the analysis, you should assume that the economy is totally market-oriented. Such an economy is sometimes referred to as a *price system.* The process by which the prices are determined is known as the *market mechanism.* The two elements of the market mechanism are *demand* and *supply.*

Demand. Think of *demand* as a series of price-quantity combinations that show the quantities of goods and services that buyers are willing and able to purchase at various prices at a given time. Several words in this definition must be noted carefully. For instance, demand is for a *series* of price-quantity combinations, not a single quantity nor a single price. The term *demand* always refers to a schedule.* For demand to take place, a consumer must be both *willing* and *able* to buy. The mere fact that a person might like to buy a new automobile does not mean that he or she has a demand for it. He or she must also be *able* to back up his or her desire with the actual money. Further, note that demand refers to purchases at a *given period of time.* As time changes, so may the series of price-quantity combinations. Think of the fads that come and go. For example, in the late fifties, there was a tremendous craze for Hula-hoops in the United States with a resultant high demand for the hoops. Today that demand has all but disappeared.

An individual's demand for a product refers to what that person stands ready to buy at each of the possible prices for that product. Such a schedule is an *individual demand schedule.* All the separate individual demands for a particular product at all

---

*Do not confuse *demand* with the term *quantity demanded,* which is the actual quantity that will be purchased at a given price.

A Model for Analyzing an Economic System

possible prices added together gives the *market demand schedule* for that particular product.

Demand Schedule and Demand Curve. The relationship between price and quantity demanded is *inverse* for most goods. As the price decreases, the quantity demanded increases and vice versa. This relationship between price and quantity demanded is called the *law of demand*. This relationship is illustrated by the schedule in table 3-1 and the demand curve shown in figure 3-5. (The data in table 3-1 may be graphed as shown in figure 3-5.)

Table 3-1. *Individual demand schedule.*

Price Per Egg	Quantity Demanded
6 cents	10
8 cents	8
10 cents	6
12 cents	4
14 cents	2

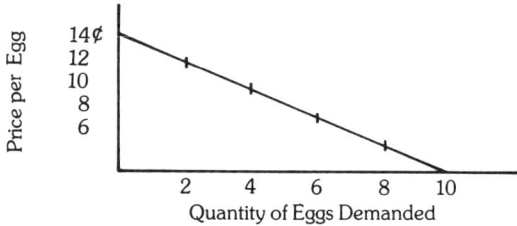

Figure 3-5. *Quantity of eggs demanded.*

Figure 3-5 is an illustration of an individual's demand for eggs. The *market demand* for eggs is merely the total of all individual demands for eggs.

If certain conditions change, then there will be changes in the demand schedule itself, independent of (or together with) price changes. The five main influences or determinants of demand are:

1. *Consumer preferences or tastes.* Over a period of time, the likes and dislikes of the buying public may change.
2. *Consumer incomes.* The amount of money a person has to spend on a particular product influences his or her demand for that good.
3. *Consumer expectations.* Whether or not the consumer thinks that the price of the product will increase or decrease in the future influences demand.
4. *Prices of other products.* The price of other products may either (a) increase demand or (b) decrease demand. Some products, for instance, go together. They are *complementary*. An example would be bread and butter or pen and ink. When the consumption of one increases, so does the consumption of the other. Two products might, however, be competitive—for example, buses and taxis. Such goods are related as *substitutes*. As taxi fares increase, the demand for bus travel goes up and vice versa.
5. *The number of consumers in the market.* The number of people competing for the goods and services available at a given time influences demand.

A Model for Analyzing an Economic System

Supply. Think of *supply* as being a series of price-quantity combinations that indicate the quantity that sellers are willing and able to offer for sale at various prices at a given period of time.

Several words in this definition should be noted carefully. Note that supply is a *series* of price-quantity combinations and not a single quantity or price. Note also that supply, like demand, refers to both a *willingness* and *ability* to offer the goods for sale. Supply, too, refers to sales *at a given period of time*. Supply, like demand, will change with the passage of time. To a business firm, the supply of a product represents a potential cost.

As the price of a product increases, the quantity supplied will tend to increase. This *direct* relationship between the increase in the quantity supplied as the price increases is called the *law of supply*.

This principle may be illustrated by the hypothetical supply schedule for a firm that produces shoes, shown in table 3–2.

Table 3–2.

Price Per Pair of Shoes	Quantity Offered for Sale
$50	500
$40	400
$30	300
$20	200
$10	100

From the data in table 3–2, a supply curve can be drawn (figure 3–6).

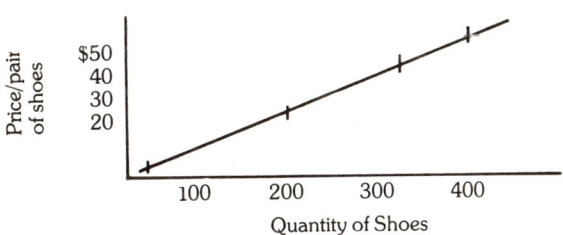

Figure 3–6. *Quantity offered for sale at specified prices.*

There are five basic determinants of supply:

1. *The technology available.* The production possibilities of a product, and therefore its supply, increase when production is highly efficient.
2. *The price of other products.* The price of other products available will influence the supply of a particular product. As was the case for demand, the price of other products can either (a) increase supply or (b) decrease supply. Some products, for example, are competitive. Assume that a farmer can grow corn or raise cattle but cannot do both. If the price of cattle increases, the farmer might shift from corn production to raising cattle. In this instance, the two products are *competitive*. Certain products are, however,

complementary. If the price of steak increases, it is not possible to supply more steak without increasing the supply of the many other cuts of meat as well.
3. *Resource prices.* The price that a producer has to pay for the land, labor, and capital needed to produce a particular product will influence the amount he or she is willing to supply.
4. *Producer expectation.* If a producer expects prices to rise in the future, he or she might withhold part or all of the supply from the market at present. The reverse would be true if the producer expected a decline in the market place.
5. *The number of producers in the market.* Supply is influenced by the number of producers competing in a given market.

Equilibrium Price. Equilibrium price is that which produces a balance between the quantity demanded and the quantity supplied. The interaction of supply and demand is illustrated in figure 3–7. Note that prices are marked along the vertical axis and the quantity demanded and the quantity supplied is marked along the horizontal axis.

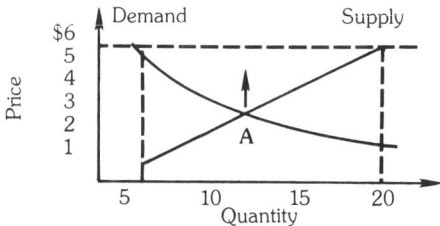

Figure 3–7. *Quantity demanded and supplied.*

Assume that in a given period of time, the price for a particular product is $5. Now examine figure 3–7 to see how the quantity demanded and the quantity supplied would be affected at this price. Note that at the price of $5, suppliers are willing to supply 20 units. However, buyers are willing to purchase only 5 units. Therefore, competition among the sellers will tend to pull prices down.

Referring again to figure 3–7, assume that a price of $1 exists for the product at a particular moment in time. Note that at this price buyers are willing to purchase 20 units of the product, but sellers are willing to supply only 5. Under this situation, competition among the buyers will tend to pull the price up.

It is only at point A in figure 3–7 that the market is in equilibrium. At this point, the quantity demanded equals the quantity supplied. This is the point where the demand curve and the supply curve intersect. At the equilibrium price, all the buyers who are willing and able to buy can find sellers who are willing and able to sell. Prices stabilize at the equilibrium point since there are no unsatisfied buyers or sellers.

Changes in Demand and Supply. Quite often beginning students in economics confuse a change in the quantity demanded or quantity supplied with a change in demand or supply. If you examine figure 3–8 closely, you will not make this mistake.

A Model for Analyzing an Economic System

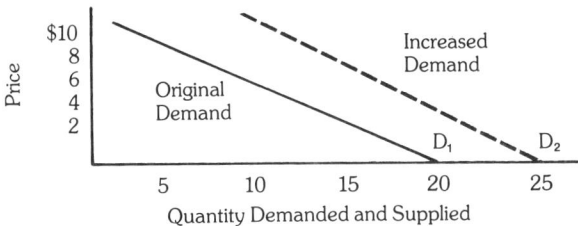

Figure 3–8. *An increase in demand.*

In figure 3–8, note the line that is labeled the "original demand" curve. This line is called the *demand schedule* or the *demand curve* or simply *demand* for short. Note that for every price along the demand curve, a different quantity is demanded. Thus changes in the quantity demanded, due to changes in price, are shown by movement along the same demand curve. There is a *change in demand* only when the entire curve shifts either to the right or to the left. An increase in demand is illustrated by a shift of the entire curve to the right, as illustrated in figure 3–8. Note that for each price along this line, there is a different quantity demanded. The quantity demanded changes as you move along the demand curve. Demand, however, changes only when the entire curve shifts. A similar line of reasoning holds true for supply considerations.

A shift in the demand for a product, or a shift in the supply of a product, usually results when there is a change in one of the demand or supply determinants, whereas a change in the quantity demanded or supplied is due to a change in the price of the product itself, other factors remaining constant.

In figure 3–9, an increase in demand is illustrated while supply is held constant.

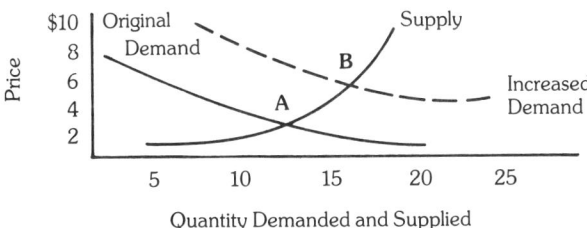

Figure 3–9. *A change in equilibrium points when demand increases.*

The original equilibrium point in figure 3–9 is indicated by point A, which is the intersection of the indicated original demand curve and the original supply curve. Note that when demand shifted to the right, the equilibrium point was shifted to Point B, which is the intersection of the original supply curve wth the new demand curve. As you can see, an increase in demand without a corresponding increase in supply raises the equilibrium price. Similarly, an increase in supply, a movement of the supply curve to the right, would decrease the price if there was not a corresponding shift in demand; this situation is illustrated in figure 3–10.

A Model for Analyzing an Economic System

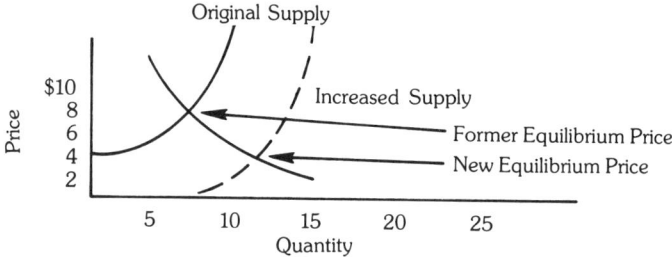

Figure 3-10. *A change in equilibrium prices when supply increases.*

A knowledge of supply and demand shifts is needed to understand changes in the price structure of a market economy.

Price Elasticity. In the preceding discussion demand and supply curves have different shapes. Underlying these differences is an important concept that is particularly of concern to business. The shape of the demand curve may be used to indicate (although not very precisely) the response of quantity demanded to changes in price. The precise measure that economists have developed to show how the quantity bought or sold responds to changes in price is called the *price elasticity of demand.*

Elasticity of demand may be defined as the degree of responsiveness of the quantity demanded to a change in price. When consumers are exceptionally responsive to small changes in price, we say the demand for the product is elastic. For example, if a corporate security (stock) is listed on two stock exchanges, a very small shift in price on one stock exchange will cause buying on one stock exchange and selling on the other. However, if the demand or supply is inelastic, the quantities demanded or supplied are less affected by price changes. For example, an increase in price of table salt does not usually result in a proportional decrease in demand for table salt. Stated more exactly, an elastic demand or supply is one in which a given percentage change in price brings about a larger percentage change in the quantity demanded or supplied.

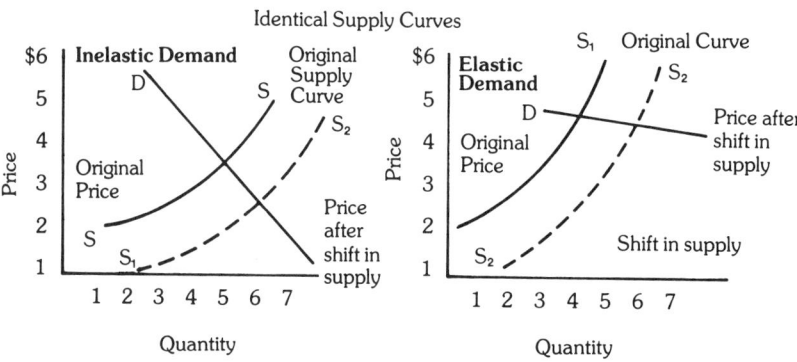

Figure 3-11. *Elastic and inelastic demand.*

Note that in figure 3-11, two identical supply curves are presented but matched with two demand curves of different slopes. In the graph on the left, the demand curve represents a highly inelastic demand. In the graph on the right, the demand curve represents a highly elastic demand. Holding the demand curves constant, assume an equal shift in supply for both illustrations. Note that for the inelastic demand curve, a shift in supply to the right (an increase in supply) created a much lower new price. However, only a slightly lower price was established for the situation where the elasticity was greater.

The market realities of price elasticity are easy to note. For example, if the demand for a product is relatively elastic and the seller cuts the price, the seller will take in more revenue. On the other hand, if the demand for a product is relatively inelastic and the seller cuts the price, revenue will fall.

Products tend to have an inelastic demand when there is no suitable substitute for them. The services of a doctor needed immediately following an accident would be an example.

The Model Completed

You are now at the point where you can, with very little additional effort, complete the model of the economy. You need only to add supply and demand considerations to the topics discussed in chapter 2, namely, problems of society, basic economic goals, and public policies. The result of these additions is shown in figure 3–12.

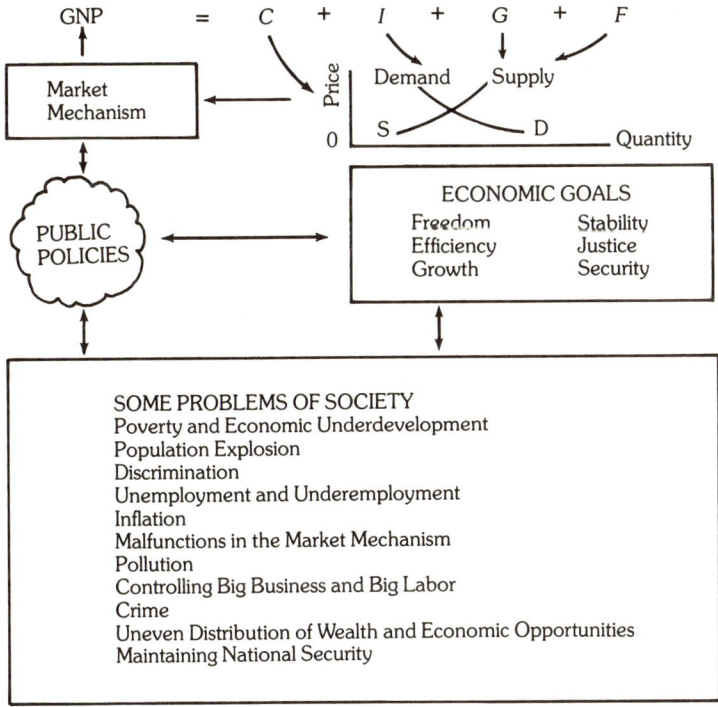

Figure 3–12. *Conceptual model for analyzing an economic system.*

Note that the spending decisions made by consumers (C), business firms (I), government (G), and the net foreign transactions (F) form the supply and demand for all goods and services produced. The prices and quantity that result from the interaction of supply and demand are reflected in the market mechanism. The total money value of all goods and services produced in the economy over a given period of time becomes the GNP.

Note that the model presented in figure 3–12 is appropriate for describing and analyzing a mixed economy. The model presents an overview of an economic *system*. A *system* is an orderly way to combine interacting component parts to form a whole. By way of analogy, an automobile is a system consisting of engine, a body, a suspension mechanism, and the like. A carburetor is a subsystem of a large transportation system.

Until we added the problems of society, basic economic goals, and public policy, our model for the economic system was that of a totally market-oriented economy. The additions, however, make it possible to analyze a mixed economy. The GNP that results from a free interaction of supply and demand is, at times, moderated through public policy to reflect the objectives of society and the intermediate economic goals. The model presented in figure 3–12 makes system analysis possible.

The model makes it possible for us to analyze certain basic economic and social relationships. In a mixed economy, public policies affect and are affected by a general belief in the market mechanism as an efficient allocator of goods and services. For example, we can trace through the model several tentative possibilities for controlling the pollution that is the result of automobile exhaust fumes. An individual consumer—represented by C in the model—could insist that before purchasing an automobile that pollution control devices be installed. In this case, the person would increase his or her personal cost. An automobile manufacturer—represented by I—could refuse to produce any automobile in which the adverse pollution effects were not tightly controlled. In this case, the producer, would increase production costs. In each of these examples, the GNP would increase since the total cost of production and the prices created through the market mechanism would increase.

Another approach to the problem would be to have the government take action through public policy making exhaust control mandatory for automobile manufacturers. Indeed, such an action was taken in 1971 by the federal government of the United States. Automobile manufacturers were given until 1976 to make the modifications specified. This action illustrates the interaction among problems of society, economic goals, and the market mechanism. Manufacturers were given a time period to adjust the new regulations so that economic growth would not be hampered severely. In the past, automobile manufacturers were able to produce whatever type of exhaust system consumers were willing to purchase. Their freedom is now curtailed to producing only that type of exhaust mechanism that meets the pollution control specifications of the government. The action also illustrates the fact that the control of pollution, in this instance, was done through public regulation of private business rather than through public ownership of private business. For instance, the U.S. government could have taken control of the automobile industry to enforce its regulations. However, a fundamental belief in the market mechanism resulted in the action taken.

The descriptive model of economics introduced in chapter 2 and completed in this chapter provides the background for circular flow analysis which will be introduced in the following chapter.

four

Circular Flow Analysis

In chapter 2, you were introduced to a descriptive model of economics. The model presented in chapter 3 outlines the content of economics and related subject matter. In a sense, it puts a fence around the body of content called economics. In this chapter, you will learn more about circular flow analysis, which is basically a dynamic and predictive model. You can use circular flow analysis to determine how the economy will function under given conditions.

Circular flow analysis is a tool to analyze the content of economics. It is a basic instrument in the economist's tool kit. Analogously, the stethoscope is one of the tools used by a doctor. The stethoscope in itself is not medicine, but it helps to make medical predictions possible. In a like manner, circular flow analysis helps to make economic predictions possible.

In this chapter, you find the answers to these questions:

1. How do savings and investments affect economic activity?
2. How does government spending and taxing affect economic activity?
3. How do exports and imports affect economic activity?
4. What is meant by the multiplier effect?

The Circular Flow of Goods and Services and the Flow of Money

The circular flow of goods and services and the flow of money are illustrated in figure 4-1. The word *flow* is used here to mean a continuous movement of goods and services and money payments.

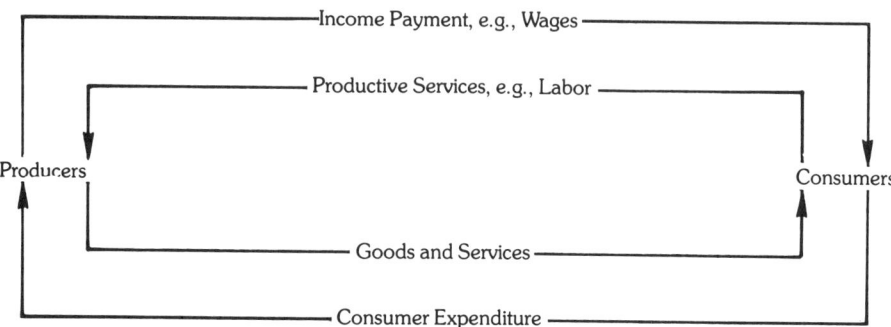

Figure 4-1. *The circular flow of goods and services and the flow of money.*

In figure 4-1 note that there are two basic economic components: (1) consumers (or households) and (2) producers (or business firms).

Every person is a consumer. Even the smallest child has needs and wants that must be satisfied. However, not all consumers are producers. Some consumers are too young, too old, or too feeble to be producers. Therefore, the producers of a society must not only satisfy their own needs and wants; they must also produce for those who are unable to produce for themselves.

Members of households (consumers) provide certain *factors of production* (such as labor) to producers who operate the business firms. Other factors of production are land, capital, and entrepreneurial (managerial) skill. The business firm combines the labor of workers with capital goods and land to produce goods and services. Those goods and services are returned to the consumers for their use. In exchange for the productive services provided by members of households, business firms make *income payments*. The reward for each of the factors of production is called by a different name.

Factors of Production	*Reward or Payments*
Labor	Wages or Salary
Land	Rent
Capital	Interest
Entrepreneurs	Profit (including dividends)

Consumers, in turn, make money payments called *consumer expenditures* to the business firms in exchange for goods and services they receive. Thus, there is a circular flow of goods and services and a circular flow of money.

As noted in chapter 3, the formula for the Gross National Product (GNP) is generally expressed in the following equation:

$$GNP = C + I + G + F$$

Circular flow analysis is especially helpful for analyzing the components of the Gross National Product.

The Effect of Savings and Investment on Economic Activity

The circular flow with which you are already familiar is presented in figure 4–2 with one modification: not all the income received by the households is spent on consumption expenditure.

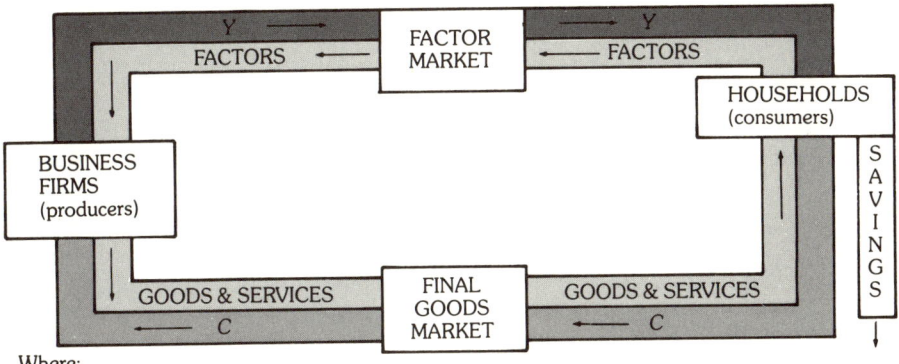

Where:
    C = Consumer Expenditures
    Y = Income Payments to Factors

Figure 4–2. *Circular flow including savings.*

Part of the income is saved. In economics, the *savings* has a very simple definition: current income received that is not spent. You should note, however, that savings refer to the *current* money set aside by consumers from their incomes, not money that has been set aside in the past. Keep in mind constantly that in flow analysis we are dealing with flows in a current time period rather than any previous accumulation of goods or money.

The commonly used symbol for income in economics is Y. In figure 4–2, we can, therefore, state the relationship of income to consumption and savings (S) by the following simple formula: $Y = C + S$.

As you will note from figure 4–2, savings are greater than zero. What effect does this have on the general level of economic activity? Since savings are greater than zero, income (Y) must be greater than consumption (C). This means that the firm pays out more to households (Y) than it receives from households in the form of their consumption (C). In other words, the firm's cost in the factor's market is greater than its income from the product's market.

The firm is paying more for labor, land, capital, and management than it is receiving in the final goods market from consumer expenditures. There is an excess of products. The firm can (1) reduce its prices or (2) reduce its production of goods and services to the point where it is equal to consumer expenditures.

If the first alternative is chosen, the firm is acting on the assumption that a lowering of prices will lead to an increase in quantity demanded and thus the surplus product could be sold. In a number of cases, a choice of the first alternative will lower the firm's profit. Since the firm's profit—including dividends—is a part of income (Y), this flow will contract. If the firm chooses the second alternative, it has to cut back on its labor, capital, and other resource costs. This action will also result in the contraction of the income flow (Y) to the household. Generally, business firms will use a combination of both alternatives. The effect is, however, basically the same. Either by cutting prices or by employing fewer resources (factors), the income flow (Y) from the business firms to the households is contracted.

When members of the household are confronted with a lower income, they must adjust their current spending and saving patterns accordingly. Your first thought might be to expect savings to be curtailed rather immediately as a result of reduced income. This is not, however, necessarily so since there is no reason to assume that the individuals whose incomes are decreased are those who were doing the saving. Consequently, it is reasonable to assume that even though savings might diminish somewhat, the major impact will be on consumer spending. Such a reaction creates another round of adjustments of the business firm. Once again the business firm will be faced with the situation where its receipts are less than its income. Once again the business firm will either lower its prices or employ fewer resources to match its cost with its revenue. The households, in turn, facing reduced income, must once again adjust to the situation.

Under the conditions presented here, how long will the downward spiral of the economy last? A solution will not come about until we return once again to a situation where $Y = C$. Under this condition, S is now equal to zero and the total output of the business firms is being purchased by the households.

Investment

The discussion to this point seems to indicate that savings have a totally depressing effect on the economy. Happily there is another side to savings. Most consumers do not put away their savings in a pillow or bury their money in the garden. When this is done, the process is called *hoarding,* not saving. Generally, people put their money in banks and other financial institutions which, in turn, make these funds available to business firms for investments.

The term *investment* refers to the purchase of capital goods—goods used to produce other goods. An increase in investment (or capital stock) is the main way that an economy can grow. Whereas savings represent a leakage from the circular flow, the counterpart, investment is an injection into it. The role of investment in circular flow analysis is illustrated in figure 4–3.

The injection of investment funds allows a business firm to produce more goods and services. In order to produce the additional goods and services, the business firm employs more resources in the factor market—market for labor, capital, and other resources. As a result, the income flowing to the household increases.

Once the additional new income arrives at the household, the individual consumer can either save this additional (marginal) income or spend it. Usually consum-

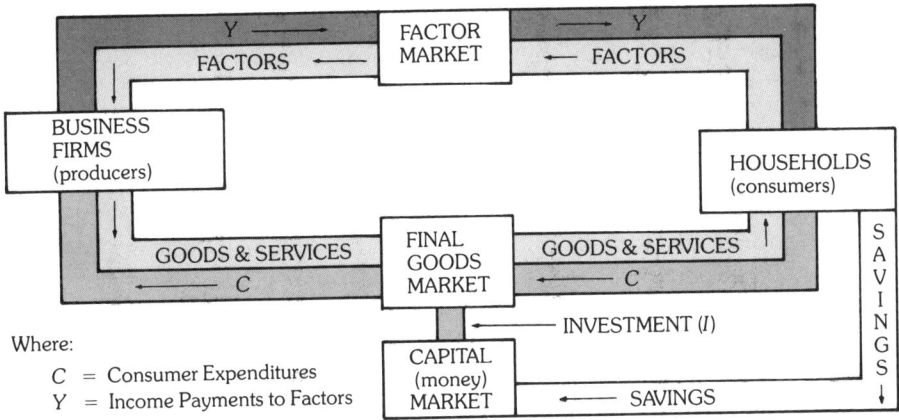

Figure 4–3. *Circular flow including investment.*

ers do a combination of both. Remember that we are talking about the additional or marginal income received by the consumer. We are assuming that the former expenditure-saving pattern continues as it was.

Assume, for example, that the average consumer chooses to spend 90 percent of his or her additional or marginal income and saves the other 10 percent. We call the fraction of new incomes consumed the *marginal propensity to consume* (often abbreviated as Mpc), or $\Delta C/\Delta Y$. We call the fractional new income that is saved the *marginal propensity to save* (often abbreviated as Mps), or $\Delta S/\Delta Y$. Or, stated in simple equation form, the propensities in our illustration are as follows: Mpc = .90 and Mps = 10.

The marginal propensity to save is always the complement of the marginal propensity to consume. For example, if the marginal propensity to consume is 80 percent (or .80), the marginal propensity to save is 20 percent (or .20).

As you will recall, the proportion of the additional income that the consumer saves will have a depressing effect upon the economic activity. The additional income the consumer chooses to spend, however, will have a stimulating effect upon economic activity. Note that in figure 4–3, savings is not shaded since it becomes part of investment (*I*) when it enters the flow through the capital money market. We must be careful not to count any items twice. Therefore, when an item—like *S*—is not shaded, it simply means that it has already been included as a part of one of the other flows.

Returning to our example, assume that the households spend 90 percent of the new income generated by the investment. The increase in spending will flow to the business firms. As a result, the business firms' revenue is greater than their costs. The firms can respond in two ways: (1) increase prices or (2) produce more goods and services. If they increase prices, this might result in greater profit—including dividends—flowing to the households. If they choose the second alternative and produce additional goods and services, they will need to employ more labor, capital, and other resources. Either course of action increases the income flow to the households.

If the households continue to spend 90 percent of the increase in income on each round and save 10 percent, can we predict the total stimulating effect on the economy? The answer is yes, we can. Simply stated, the multiplier effect is determined by the reciprocal of the marginal propensity to save. First, put the marginal propensity to save in fraction form. If, for example, the households on the average save 10 percent of all new income, write this as 1/10. If they save 50 percent of their marginal income, write this as 1/2. If they save 25 percent of the marginal income, write this as 1/4. The multiplier may now be determined simply by taking the reciprocal of the marginal propensity to save. If consumers save 1/10 of their marginal income, the multiplier effect would be 10 assuming no leakage, say increased income spent on imports or increased taxes. Obviously, the stimulation to the economy comes about from the amount spent rather than the amount saved. We use the marginal propensity to save simply because it is the complement of the marginal propensity to consume. The extra consumption is what produces the multiplier effect.

The equation for a multiplier is:

$$\frac{1}{1-Mpc} \text{ or } \frac{1}{Mps}$$

Thus, if the marginal propensity to consume is 3/4, then the multiplier will be:

$$\frac{1}{1-Mpc} = \frac{1}{1-3/4} = \frac{1}{1/4} = 4$$

Thus, if initially there were an increase in income of $5, then given a Mpc of 3/4 we would have a multiplier effect of 4 and, therefore, total income would increase by $20. The actual process by which this takes place may be demonstrated as shown in table 4–1. Remember that underlying the multiplier effect is the fact that one person's expenditure is another person's income.

Table 4–1.

	Change in Incomes	Change in Consumption (Mpc =3/4)	Change in Saving (Mps =1/4)
First Round Initial increase in income of Consumer A	$5.00	$3.75	$1.25
Second Round Expenditure of A is income of B	3.75	2.81	.94
Third Round Expenditure of B is income of C	2.81	2.11	.70
All others	8.44	6.33	2.11
TOTAL	$20.00	$15.00	$5.00

Investments serve as injections into the economy and stimulate economic activity. They create continuing rounds of increased production, employment, income, and so forth. When would we want to halt such an upward spiral? The answer is that we would want to halt such activity at such time as all the resources are totally employed. Once all the factors—land, labor, capital, and management—are being used to full capacity, then further injections into the economy merely result in increased prices. The multiplier, as we have noted thus far, relates changes in real income to changes in spending and saving or a change in investment to a change in real income. However, when we have full employment, the multiplier effect will lead to increases in money income and not real income. To distinguish between these two forms of the multiplier effect, economists call the former the *employment multiplier* and the latter the *income mutiplier*. The change in real income is referred to as the employment multiplier because when there is a real expansion of output, there is an increase in employment (or other factors) as well.

There is, of course, a direct relationship between savings and investments. When savings exceed investments, the depressing effect of the savings will more than offset the stimulating effect of investments. When investments exceed savings, the stimulating effect of the investments will more than offset the depressing effect of savings. Economic stability exists when savings are equal to investments.

The Role of Earnings and Depreciation

Like consumers, producers either spend or save the money they receive. The amount that they save or retain in the business firm is called *retained earnings*. Retained earnings refer to a portion of profits which *could have been* distributed to the households. For that reason, retained earnings are generally considered to be a part of total income (Y) since the total income includes the returns to all factors of production. Total income includes all wages, rent, interest, and profits. Note that retained earnings is not shaded in figure 4–4 as it is assumed to be a part of Y since it could have been distributed to households and is considered to be a part of total income.

Business firms also put money into the capital (money) market by making allowances for depreciation. Tools, machines, and other capital goods do wear out in time. Money that is set aside to replace equipment is called either *depreciation* or *capital consumption allowances*. Depreciation is *not* a part of the total income (Y) since it is not a factor payment. Rather, it is simply a business expense. The role of retained earnings and depreciation is illustrated in figure 4–4.

For analysis, recall that retained earnings and personal savings have not been shaded. The reason for this is that they have already been counted as part of Y—the flow labeled "money income." Depreciation, however, is shaded since it is a cost of doing business that is not a part of Y. Part of the S flow also reenters the shaded portion of the circular flow as I.

Since the circular flow diagram presented in figure 4–4 does not include government or foreign trade, note that GNP can be determined by either the expenditure or the cost method: $GNP = C + I$ (the expenditure method) or $GNP = Y + D$ (the cost method).

Circular Flow Analysis

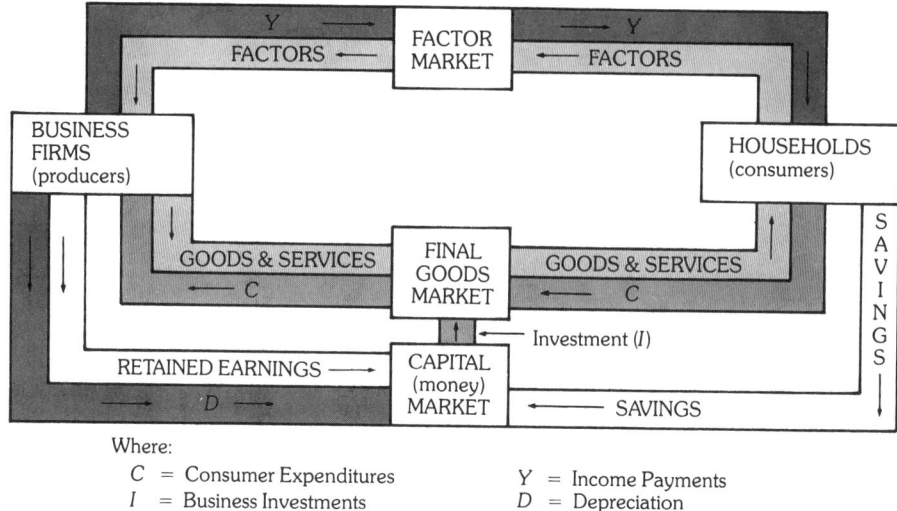

Where:
C = Consumer Expenditures
I = Business Investments
Y = Income Payments
D = Depreciation

Figure 4-4. *Circular flow including depreciation.*

Remember that Y stands for all payments to the factors of production (wages, rent, interest, and profits) and D stands for depreciation.

The Effect of Government Taxing and Spending on Economic Activity

You are now ready to add an extremely important component to the circular flow diagram, namely government. In the United States, for instance, the government (local, state, and national) generates about 23 percent of the GNP. The economic role of the government consists of (1) taxing and (2) spending. These two activities have been added to the circular flow presented in figure 4–5 and will be explained in the section that follows.

Taxing

Any form of government taxation has a depressing effect on economic activity. Taxation represents a leakage in the circular flow. Consider the case of an income tax. If households must pay an income tax, they have less money available to either spend or save. Consequently, taxes reduce the general level of aggregate (total) demand. Since, as a result of taxation, households have less money to spend for consumer goods and services, the business firms will adjust accordingly. As you will recall from your previous analysis, the business firm will reduce either its prices or its output or both. A reduction in prices will lead to lower profits (including dividends) being distributed to the households. A reduction in output will lead to a reduction in the employment of the factors of production. Consequently, in either case the money income (Y) flowing to the households will be reduced.

Taxation, therefore, exerts a depressing effect on the economy and brings about a downward spiral of economic activity.

Note that in figure 4–5, government taxes are either (1) direct or (2) indirect.

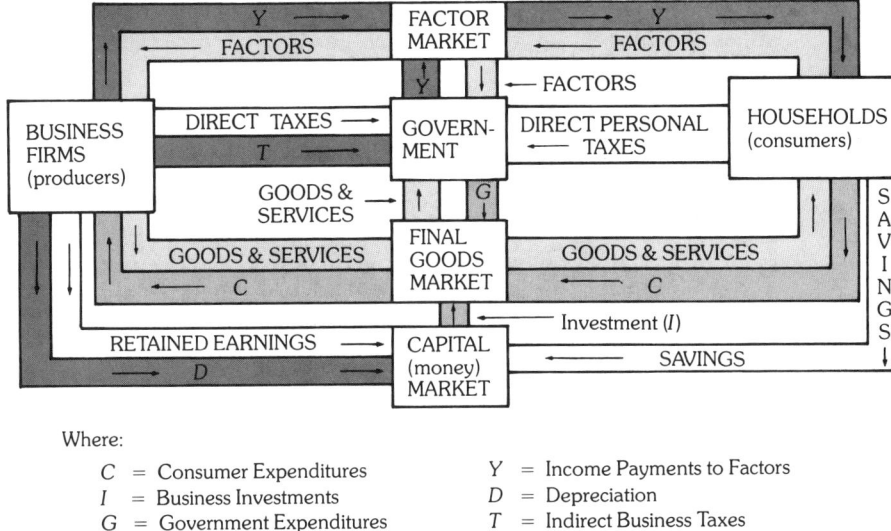

Where:

C = Consumer Expenditures
I = Business Investments
G = Government Expenditures
Y = Income Payments to Factors
D = Depreciation
T = Indirect Business Taxes

Figure 4–5. *The role of government.*

Direct Taxes

The direct taxes are either (1) direct business taxes or (2) direct personal taxes.

In both cases, these are taxes on incomes. They relate directly to the employment of the factors of production. They are factor costs. A business firm pays a direct tax only when (and if) it earns a profit. The tax is not a cost of doing business; rather, it is the result of doing business. The same line of reasoning relates to direct personal taxes. These taxes are paid only when and if a household earns income. These taxes are not a cost of earning the income; they are the result of earning the income. Stated in another way, direct taxes come about as a result of the government's extracting part of the income that would normally go to a factor of production. Households would have more income if there were no direct personal taxes. Business firms would have more profits (that could be distributed to the households) if there were no direct business taxes. For this reason, the direct taxes are not shaded in figure 4–5. The amount of the direct taxes have already been included in Y. Recall that Y equals the total flow of money income to the factors, including retained business earnings. It is, therefore, appropriate that all direct taxes be considered a part of the Y flow. You could, of course, peel off part of the money income flow and illustrate it as flowing to the government. For simplicity, however, we have shown all direct taxes *without* shading. The money that the taxes represent remains in the flow labeled Y, or money income.

Indirect Taxes

Note that indirect taxes, labeled T, are shaded. The reason for this is that these taxes are not picked up in the Y flow. Recall that Y represents the total cost of *employing the factors of production*. Nonetheless, indirect taxes are a definite *cost* of doing business. They are not levied on factors of production, but rather on the productive enterprise itself or on its actual physical product. Examples of indirect taxes would include real estate taxes, taxes that are levied on each unit of output whether or not the product is sold (such as a cigarette tax), or taxes levied on goods sold at retail (sales tax). All taxes of this type are payments made by business firms as a cost of doing business.

The total cost of production as illustrated in figure 4-5 (which does not include foreign trade) includes factor costs (Y), depreciation (D), and indirect business taxes (T). Therefore, if you wish to determine the GNP by the cost-of-production method, you can do so simply by applying the following formula: GNP = Y + D + T (all shaded the same). These flows—Y, D, and T—represent the *aggregate supply*.

Spending

At this point, taxation appears to have a totally depressing effect on the economy. However, government taxing is done in order to provide certain government services through spending. Keep in mind that government spending occurs at all levels: local, state, and national.

Government spending consists of (1) direct spending and (2) transfer payments. Direct spending refers to the actual purchase of goods and services by the government. For example, if a government builds a highway, constructs a school, or employs a teacher, there is a direct purchase of a good or a service. Such purchases, in turn, directly affect the GNP.

The government also engages in another type of spending activity, which is quite different from the direct purchase of goods and services. This type of spending involves *transfer payments*. Transfer payments refer to money collected through taxes from one source and distributed to another source. No goods or services are actually purchased in the process. Welfare payments provide an example. Such payments merely redistribute income among the citizens of a nation. Transfer payments are neither a leakage nor an injection into the circular flow. Consequently, payments of this type are not included in figure 4-5 nor do they affect aggregate economic analysis, except in that they redistribute income among citizens.*

When the government purchases goods and services, however, there is a direct and immediate effect upon the GNP. For simplicity of analysis, we assume in figure 4-5 that the government purchases all of its goods and services from business firms. In reality, the government actually produces many goods and services itself. In such cases, however, the government is essentially acting as a business firm. For that reason, in figure 4-5, we have not shaded the flow representing the payment of the factors of production that are used by the government. The money income received by all factors of production is assumed to be represented in Y, the flow of money income. An arrow has been drawn from the factors markets to government merely to remind you that the government does employ factors of production. The actual

---

*Since redistribution of income is usually from richer people to poorer people, the redistribution might affect savings rates, which in turn might affect aggregate economic analysis. These refinements are, however, left to more advanced analysis.

production, however, in our illustration takes place in the component labeled "business firms" (producers).

We have shaded the government expenditures that flow *from* the final goods market. Our reason for doing this is to separate government expenditures from consumption expenditures. We wish to show that aggregate demand consists of consumer expenditures (C), business investments (I), and government expenditures (G).

Government spending for goods and services has a stimulating effect on the general level of economic activity. It adds to the aggregate demand for goods and services. When the government purchases goods and services, money is pumped into the economy.

When the additional funds pumped into the economy by government spending reach the business firms (producers), the firms will react in one of three ways: they will increase prices, increase output, or both. If the total resource capacity (land, labor, capital, and management) is fully employed, added government spending will merely drive prices upward. Under such a situation, increased production would be impossible. The government would simply have to pay higher prices in order to divert some of the production to its use.

In most instances, however, the productive capacity of a nation is not fully employed. When this is the case, government purchasing of goods and services generates additional output. Business firms (or the government itself when acting as a producer) employ additional factors (land, labor, capital, and management) to produce the additional output generated.

Whether government spending results in higher prices, increased output, or a combination of these, the flow of income payments to the households increases. Higher prices would generate increased profits—including dividends—that would flow to the households. If output is increased, the households would receive greater income in the form of wages, interest, rent, and profits. When the households receive the additional income, they can either (1) spend it or (2) save it. Usually, some combination of these two alternatives will be adopted. In fact, we can generally predict with a great deal of accuracy what percentage of the additional (marginal) income will be spent and what percentage will be saved. Recall that the percentage of additional income received that is spent on consumption is called the marginal propensity to consume, or Mpc for short. The percentage of additional income that is saved is called marginal propensity to save, or Mps. The marginal propensity to consume for the American society was extremely stable over time, running at about 92 to 93 percent until the late 1970s, when it increased to as much as 96% as a result of a savings decline during the recession. Consequently, this means that the marginal propensity to save must be less than 10 percent. Assume for a moment that the Mps is 10 percent. Recall that the multiplier is the reciprocal of the fraction represented by saving. Therefore, savings would be 1/10 of the additional income. It then follows that the multiplier would be 10. Consequently, an injection of government spending of one billion dollars would bring about a ten-billion-dollar increase in total income as the spiral works its way through the economy.

In fact, the actual multiplier that is created by government spending is much less. The reason for this is that there are leakages other than savings. The total consumer spending of the additional income is much less than the 90 percent used in our example. Part of the additional income must be paid in taxes. The combined federal, state, and local taxes in countries such as the United States represents about 40 percent of the marginal income. Also, the additional income created through government spending makes it possible for businesses to increase their savings. Generally business savings from the additional income generated in this fashion will run about 10 percent. Imports are another type of leakage that result as income rises. The higher incomes encourage additional buying abroad. For example, a family might vacation abroad or buy a foreign car or other product from another country.

Therefore, all leakages—personal savings, business savings, taxes, and imports—combine to produce a multiplier that is much less than we might guess upon first analysis. In the United States the actual multiplier is estimated to be about 2. Stated another way, government expenditures of one billion dollars will tend to increase the GNP by approximately two billion dollars.

Aggregate demand is represented by the flow of consumer spending (C), business investments (I), and government spending (G). Therefore, if you wish to determine the GNP by the expenditures method, you can do so simply by applying the following formula: GNP = C + I + G (all shaded the same).

Government Budget

The government's budget is a result of the relationship between its spending and its taxing. The budget can (1) have a surplus, (2) have a deficit, or (3) be balanced.

A Government Budget Surplus. A surplus exists when government taxing is greater than government spending. In this situation, more money is drained from the economy than is pumped in. Aggregate demand is reduced. Business firms react to the decrease in demand by reducing prices, decreasing output, or both. As a result, income and consumer expenditure spiral lower. GNP falls. Such a policy would be appropriate during an inflationary period. Note that an increase in taxes has the same effect as a decrease in government spending. A government surplus can be brought about, then, by either (a) decreasing government spending or (b) increasing taxes.

A Government Budget Deficit. A *deficit* exists when government spending is greater than its taxing. Deficits stimulate the economy by pumping additional funds into the circular flow. Aggregate demand is increased. Firms respond by either raising prices, increasing output, or both. Money income increases. Consumer expenditures expand. GNP goes up. This type of policy is appropriate when a deflationary condition exists. A deflationary period is characterized by unused and underused resources such as labor and capital. In a deflationary period, there is both unemployment and underemployment. Note that the government deficit can be brought about by either (a) increasing government spending or (b) decreasing taxes. Either approach will exert a stimulating effect upon the economy.

A Balanced Budget. A *balanced budget* exists when government spending equals its taxing. The depressing effects of taxation are offset by the stimulating effects of spending. Such a policy would be appropriate at a time of economic stability coupled with full employment.

The Effect of Foreign Trade on Economic Activity

We are now ready to add the effects foreign trade has on the general level of economic activity. Foreign, or international, trade consists of (1) imports and (2) exports.

Net foreign exports is defined as exports minus imports, and it is labeled F in our formula for GNP, which is repeated here: GNP $= C + I + G + F$. The effects of foreign trade have been added to the circular flow diagram presented in figure 4–6.

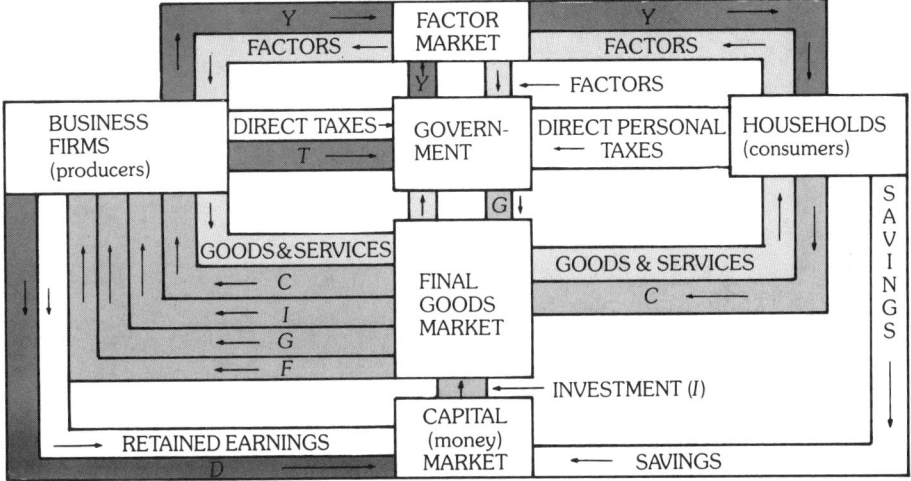

Figure 4–6. *Circular flow including foreign trade.*

Imports

Imports represent the goods and services that are purchased from foreign countries. The money paid for such goods and services leaves the domestic economy and is, therefore, a leakage in the circular flow.

Assume, for example, that households divert some of their consumer expenditures to import. For example, a person might purchase a Japanese camera or French wine. The result will be a decrease in aggregate domestic demand. Business firms will react by lowering prices, decreasing output, or both. As a result of the business firm's adjustments, the money income flow (Y) from business firms to households will contract. When incomes are reduced, consumers respond, in turn, by reducing their consumer expenditures. Imports, therefore, set about a downward spiral in economic activity.

Exports

Exports represent the goods and services that foreign buyers purchase from the domestic economy. Money spent for exports flows into the economy. It is an injection into the circular flow. Business firms respond to the increase in the money flow by raising prices, increasing output, or both. The response of the business firms

48   Circular Flow Analysis

increases the flow of money income (Y) to consumers. Consumers respond to the increase of income by increasing their consumer expenditures, savings, or a combination of both. Exports, therefore, bring about an upward spiral in the economy. Aggregate demand is increased. The GNP goes up.

If exports equalled imports, the circular flow would be unaffected. The stimulation of the economy brought about through exports would be offset by the dampening effect of imports. Aggregate demand would remain constant. GNP would not change.*

Summary of Injections and Leakages

At this point, we can summarize the economic effects of the major components of the economy. For the purpose of this summary, we will use the diagram of a bucket, as illustrated in figure 4–7.

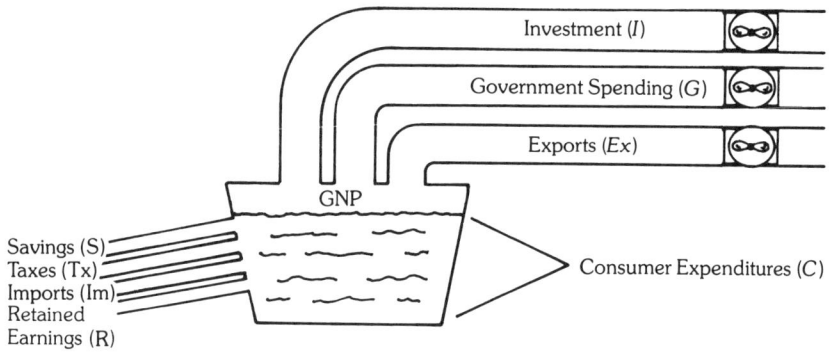

Figure 4–7. *Injections and leakages.*

Recall that consumer expenditures (C) tend to be quite constant. We, therefore, designate the "normal" flow level in the bucket to be C.

Three pipes with appropriate control valves provide injections into our bucket. Note that these injections are labeled investment (I), government spending (G), and exports (Ex). (We do not use F as our label since F is used for *net* foreign exports.)

Four drainage pipes, also with appropriate control valves, serve as drains from our bucket. These pipes represent leakages in the economy. Note that the valves are labeled savings (S), taxes (Tx), Imports (Im), and retained earnings (R). (We do not use T as our label for taxes since T is used to denote *only* indirect business taxes.)

Note also that the level of flow in the bucket has been labeled GNP. This is realistic since GNP is equal to consumer expenditures (C), plus government spending (G), and net foreign exports (F).

The GNP flow within the bucket can be adjusted by the regulation of the injection and the leakage valves. If the injection valve for government spending (G) is opened, the GNP level will rise. That situation is illustrated in figure 4–8.

---

*In this chapter, we have considered only those foreign payments which are directly tied to the production of goods and services. We shall reserve to a later discussion money transfers, foreign aid, and other expenditures which are not directly related to GNP analysis.

Circular Flow Analysis   49

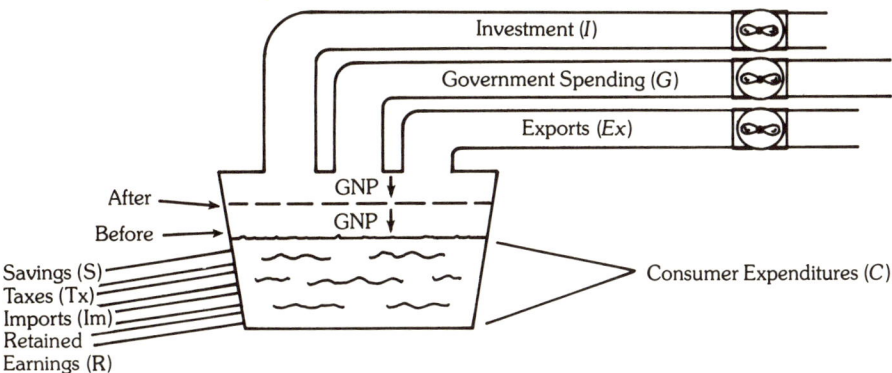

Figure 4-8.   *Adjustments to the injections and leakage valves.*

Note that GNP level rises and falls depending upon how the valves for the injection and leakage pipes are adjusted. From this analysis, you can see that the level of GNP is the result of many flows that can be combined in a number of different ways.

The next analogy, which is designed to show the role of the multiplier effect, will take a little more imagination. Assume, for example, that you turn on the valve that controls government spending. This action will raise the level of GNP. However, after you turn off the valve some flow continues. The valve is not completely tight. The flow that continues after the valve has been turned off represents the multiplier effect.

The bucket illustration serves to illustrate still one more useful concept in GNP analysis. When the bucket is completely full, all factors of production—land, labor, capital, and management—are being used at full capacity. If an additional injection is added at this point, the "real" GNP can no longer rise. The bucket will simply overflow. In an economy, the overflow of the bucket would represent inflation. A bucket that is not totally full would represent unemployment or unused resources.

As you know, GNP = C + I + G + F. We have introduced a general analysis of GNP. In the next four chapters we shall analyze the components of GNP in more detail. We shall begin our analysis in the following chapter with households and personal economics—the C in the equation for GNP.

five

The Households: Personal Economics

Chapters 5, 6, 7, and 8 are devoted to an examination of the major components of a market economy. The sequence of the subject matter to be analyzed will follow the formula: GNP $= C + I + G + F$.

In this chapter, we shall analyze the economic role of the households as consumers. In subsequent chapters the focus will be upon the business firm (I), government (G), and foreign trade (F).

The circular flow model developed in some detail in chapter 4 is not repeated in chapters 5, 6, 7, and 8. However, an excellent way to review these chapters is to return to the circular flow model presented in chapter 4 and relate the material presented to that model.

In this chapter you will find the answers to these questions:

1. What is personal economic analysis?
2. What are the economic roles performed by an individual?
3. What are the economic activities performed by an individual?
4. What is the relationship between personal economic analysis and aggregate economic analysis?
5. What is meant by the functional distribution of income?
6. What is meant by the personal distribution of income?
7. How do incomes vary by region and state in the United States?

8. How do we compare income changes over time?
9. What are price indices?
10. How can price indices be constructed and used?

Personal Economic Analysis*

Personal economic analysis is a study of how an individual earns and uses her or his income by functioning as a worker, a consumer, and a citizen.

Economic Roles of the Individual

As you know from our previous discussion, every individual is a *consumer*. Every living human being has certain needs and wants that must be fulfilled. Even an infant engages in consumption activities. Recall, however, that not all individuals are *producers (workers)*. In the United States, approximately 40 percent of the population is in the labor force. Individuals under age sixteen, retired people, homemakers, and certain other groups of people (such as those in penal institutions) are not officially counted as a part of the labor force since they do not receive an income. Those in the labor force produce the goods and services that are consumed not only by themselves, but by other people not in the labor force. Also, the citizenship role of individuals varies considerably. For some, this role is passive; for others it is very active indeed. A knowledge of economics is helpful to a person when he or she engages in the *basic economic roles* of being a (1) worker, (2) consumer, and/or (3) a citizen.

Most individuals who work do so to earn income to buy economic goods and services. Naturally, an individual wants his or her work to be satisfying as well. The real or opportunity cost of work is the leisure time foregone. Most of us strive to maintain a balance between our work and the other activities of our daily living.

As a consumer, or user of income, the individual must make certain decisions regarding spending, borrowing, savings, and investing. In an effort to maximize consumption satisfactions, the individual can (1) spend all income received, (2) borrow additional money to increase consumption, (3) save part of the income to acquire a greater amount of goods and services at a future date, or (4) invest part of the income in an attempt to increase the total income in time.

If you spend all of your income, you have made a decision that this approach will give you the greatest consumption satisfaction in your particular situation.

If you decide to borrow money to increase your consumption of goods and serivces now, you have made the decision that your greatest consumption satisfaction will be improved in this manner. Basically, you have decided to consume more now and less in the future since the money borrowed will have to be paid back at a later date. Most people who purchase a large item such as a home or an automobile find it necessary to borrow money that is paid back at a later date.

---

*Much of the material in this section of the chapter has been adapted from Roman F. Warmke and Eugene D. Wyllie, *Consumer Economic Problems,* 9th ed. (Cincinnati: South-Western Publishing Co., 1977) by permission of the publisher.

52 The Households: Personal Economics

Even if you have borrowed money, you might still wish to save part of your current income to provide for increased buying power at a future date. Most people engage in borrowing and saving at the same time. The opportunity cost of saving is to give up the pleasure of consumption now in order to be able to consume more at a later date. Or possibly, your purpose of saving might simply be to provide you with a greater sense of financial security.

If you make a decision to invest, you sacrifice the present use of income or savings in an attempt to increase your future income. In this case, the word *investment* means any expenditure of funds designed to increase future income. You should note this difference in definition carefully since it is not the same as the way the word *investment* is usually used in economics. Recall from chapter 1 that we stated that investment refers to the purchase of capital goods—goods used to produce other goods. The latter definition is the usual one used throughout this textbook. However, when we are discussing the economic roles of an individual, the term has a slightly different and broader meaning.*

As a citizen, an individual strives to maximize his or her satisfaction from public goods and services. The citizenship role is essentially one of collective decision making. The real or opportunity cost of collective decision making is to give up a certain amount of personal freedom and individual choice. For example, it is difficult (if not impossible) for the private individual to provide for schools, roads, hospitals, defense, and other types of public goods and services. Consequently, individuals act collectively and pay taxes so that these goods and services can be provided. The payment of taxes, in turn, reduces the amount of money that the individual has available for his or her private consumption decisions.

The Relationship between Personal and Aggregate Economic Analysis

The relationship between personal economic decision making and the total economy is presented in table 5–1. Note that the individual economic roles and activities are identified in the left-hand column. The decision-making process of the individual is identified along the top of the diagram. The decision-making process involves a definition of the problem and an analysis of how the decision made will affect both the individual and the total system.

---

*An individual generally thinks of the purchase of stocks and bonds as being an investment, and for the individual this is indeed true. In aggregate economic analysis, however, such an expenditure of funds would not be considered an investment since no goods or services are produced in the process. The purchase of securities from one person by another merely represents a redistribution of income or wealth within the economy—a mere transfer of claims. No additional goods or services are produced in the process. In aggregate economic analysis, the sale of business securities is viewed as an investment only at the time the securities are originally sold. At that time, and at that time only, does the sale of business securities provide new money that can be used for the purchase of capital goods. And even then the actual investment takes place only when the newly acquired funds are spent for new plants and equipment. Consequently, when you use the word *investment* you will have to designate whether you are using it in a personal economic sense or in terms of aggregate economic analysis. To repeat, when the term is used in this textbook it will be used in the aggregate economic sense unless otherwise indicated..

Table 5-1. *Personal Economics Grid*

Roles and Activities	Decision Making: Define the Problem	INDIVIDUAL LEVEL: Identify goals what BENEFITS	INDIVIDUAL LEVEL: Analyze alternatives what COSTS	Effects of the Whole System on Individual Actions	Effects of Individual Action on the Whole System
I. Worker Receiver of income; earning or receiving income	To become trained or not? What job to take? How long and how hard to work?	To provide goods or purchasing power	To expend time or effort, and to lose leisure	Scarcity of unskilled jobs suggests further education	More people working raises GNP
II. Consumer User of Income — Spending	What to buy? How much to spend? To buy or rent housing?	To satisfy wants and to acquire goods and services	To sacrifice other goods and savings	Expected inflation encourages buying now before prices rise	Fall-off in spending for durables brings on recession
Borrowing	Whether to borrow? How much? Where? Bank or finance company? At what interest rate?	To consume more now (positive time preference)	To consume less now	Low interest rates encourages present borrowing	Excessive borrowing sparks inflation
Saving	Whether to save? How much? What purchases to postpone? What future needs to be met?	To have future income or security or to finance investment (to consume more later)	To consume less now	Rising prosperity reduces need for a backlog of savings	Inadequate savings pushes interest rates up
Investing	What is the rate of return? How safe? Should savings be kept liquid?	To increase future income	To sacrifice present use of control of savings (liquidity preference)	Falling stock market suggests keeping savings liquid instead of investing	Heavy investing helps economic growth
III. Citizen Influencing regulation and allocation of public vs. private goods	What party to vote for? To contribute to party? To run for office? (What policies to support?)	To obtain for self and others the benefits of public goods and improved environment	To pay taxes or suffer inflation, and accept some loss of individual choice	Government restrictions on credit discourages home building	Willingness to pay taxes brings better roads and schools

Reprinted, with permission, from *Teaching Personal Economics in the Social Studies Curriculum* (New York: Joint Council on Economic Education, 1971), p. 13. This material may not be reproduced without special authorization from the Joint Council on Economic Education, 1212 Avenue of the Americas, New York, N.Y. 10036.

If, for example, you decide that you would like to earn additional income you must decide such questions as the following:

Do I want to become better trained or not?
What job should I take to earn additional income?
How long and hard am I willing to work?

You might decide, for instance, to become better trained in order to be able to hold the job that has a higher income. The benefit to you would be the ability to purchase additional goods and services. Your cost would be the time and effort spent on the additional training and the loss of some leisure. Note that in table 5–1, the second and third columns appear in bold type. This is to indicate that the nature of the main benefits and costs of each type of activity remains constant and is universal. The benefits and the cost are the same in the United States as they are in Europe or South America. They are the same in the twentieth century as they were in the first century. The other columns, however, contain simple examples of the questions that must be answered.

The conditions that exist within the economy will dictate to you what type of position you should pursue in order to increase your income. A shortage of unskilled jobs would suggest that you can increase your income by increasing your education. By increasing your education you might, in turn, increase your productivity which would generate additional GNP.

Frequently, what is good for the individual might not be good for the total society. For instance, at a time of anticipated increasing prices, an individual might decide that it would be to his or her advantage to spend more now and/or increase borrowing. If a number of individuals increase their spending and/or borrowing, the process might in fact bring about the expected inflation.

Sometimes, of course, individual decision making is helpful to the total economic acitivity. An individual might, for example, expect a period of prosperity and invest additional money. These investments, in turn, increase the capital stock of the nation and make it possible for a greater production of goods and services. If a number of individuals pursue the same line of reasoning, they do in fact help bring about the expected prosperity.

As a citizen, the individual might vote to increase public expenditures for better roads and schools. If unemployment exists at the time, the expenditures of public funds to improve the roads and schools might reduce unemployment. If, however, the total resources of the economy are employed, such an expenditure of funds would be inflationary since the government would have to bid higher prices to attract workers and other resources away from their present employment.

The examples given here illustrate the effects of the whole system on the individual and the effects of individual decision making on the whole system. The economic decisions made by individuals do affect the entire system. Similarly, the economic condition of the whole system affects the decisions made by individuals.

As indicated previously, an excellent way to analyze the relationship between an aggregate economic analysis and personal decision making is to trace the effect of each individual economic decision on the circular flow. As you do so, keep in mind the equation: $GNP = C + I + G + F$. For every personal economic decision, ask yourself what will happen to GNP. For instance, if an individual increases his or her consumer expenditures while all other components of the economy are held constant, GNP will expand. Keep in mind also that the multiplier effect will operate. As a review, trace through the circular flow how GNP will be affected by changes in spending, borrowing, saving, and investing.

National Income Distribution

The households of an economy are responsible for the largest share of the total demand in almost all societies. Generally the households will constitute almost two-thirds of the total demand for output. Households determine how resources will be used by their consumption decisions. More than that, households influence the capital formulation of a nation through their savings decisions. As you recall, savings are usually placed in a financial institution which, in turn, makes these funds available for business investment. Consequently, the role of households in every society is extremely important.

The household category can be subdivided into (1) families, (2) individuals living alone, and (3) private institutions. All three groups make private consumption decisions. The pattern of income distribution to the households can be viewed as either (1) functional or (2) personal.

Functional Distribution

The functional distribution of income refers to the source of that income. As you will recall, each factor of production receives money income. Labor receives wages and salaries. Property owners receive rent. People who supply the money capital to businesses receive interest. Entrepreneurs (risk takers) receive profits, including dividends. The functional distribution of income shows the source of household income according to the economic contributions made. An approximation of the functional distribution of income in the United States is illustrated in figure 5–1.

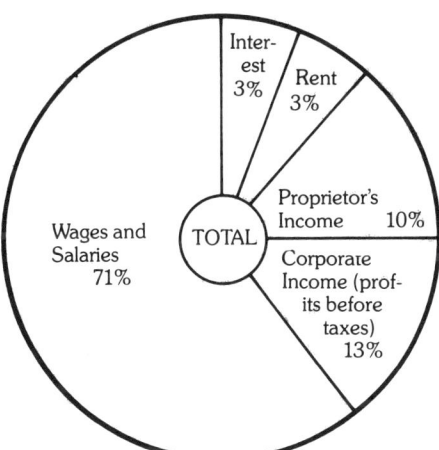

Figure 5–1. *Sources of income in the United States.*

From figure 5–1 you will note that wage and salary earners receive by far the largest share of the total national income. The next higher portion of the national income is corporate profits (before taxes) followed by proprietor's income, rents, and interest, respectively.

Personal Distribution

The personal distribution of income indicates how the total income of a nation is divided among the particular households.

In a mixed economy the personal distribution of income is important because of the way if affects the allocation of resources and capital formation. If the income is concentrated heavily in wealthy households, the demand for luxuries increases. If the income is more evenly distributed, there will be a greater demand for food, clothing, and shelter.

The pattern of income distribution also affects the amount of savings in a nation. Once again, if the income is concentrated in the hands of a few households, total savings will increase. This is true because the households with the higher incomes tend to account for most of the savings. Those households in the lower category of household income generally are not able to save much, if anything, since they need their incomes to provide for the basic needs of food, clothing, and shelter. Consequently, an uneven personal distribution of income might lead to greater saving for a nation.

Income distribution varies by geographical regions. Some sections of the world are wealthier than others. In like manner, some states within a country are wealthier than others.

Income distribution varies in geographical regions.

In the section on poverty in chapter 1 we examined the reasons that certain geographical regions are wealthier than others. The per capita income distribution of a region is directly related to the productivity of that region. For instance, the modern urban sector is generally the most productive and therefore has the highest per capita income. The traditional rural sector is generally least productive and therefore has the lowest per capita income. The geographical proximity to domestic and international markets will also affect the income of the region. The quantity and quality of transportation, communication, and other services will affect the regional income. Obviously, the kinds and availability of resources (e.g., mineral deposits) will greatly affect regional income. In addition, the income of a region is affected directly by the level of education and the technical know-how of its population. These factors help to explain why certain southern states in the United States (such as Mississippi, Alabama, and Arkansas) are relatively less wealthy than states such as Connecticut, New York, and Nevada.

The Use of Price Indices

Besides knowledge of functional and personal distribution of income, it is important to know something of the changes in income over time. Often we merely observe changes in income in terms of money figures. However, conclusions and comparisons made on the basis of money figures can be very misleading.

In order to understand the significance of changes in income data you must be familiar with the way money figures are "corrected" so that prices and incomes in one year can be compared with prices and incomes in another year. As you will recall from previous discussions, GNP measures the monetary value of all goods and services produced in a country for a year. It is quite possible that the dollar value could increase as a result of price changes while the total quantity of goods and services produced in a country for a year stayed the same or actually decreased.

The Consumer Price Index

Most countries maintain a consumer price index (CPI) to measure price changes from year to year. In round numbers, the consumer price index in 1979 for the United States was twice (200 percent) the index for 1967. What does this information tell you? First, it tells you that the year 1967 was chosen as the *base* year. Therefore, all other years are compared to the prices in 1967. In order to do this, the price index for 1967 was set at 100. The price index in 1979 was 100 percent higher (double) than the price index of 1967.

The consumer price index itself refers to a typical "basket" of goods and services purchased by the citizens of a nation. In the United States, some 400 basic commodities and services are included in the index. Categories include food, clothing, rent, transportation, medical care, and other items. The same "basket" of goods and services is checked year by year for price changes. These changes are noted in the calculation of the new consumer price index. Using 1967 as the base year (giving it an index of 100), consumer price changes as measured by the CPI have changed from that date as follows:

Year	CPI
1967	100
1970	116
1975	162
1979	217

(preliminary data, August 1979)

Assume, for example, that your income for a given period of time in 1967 was $1,000. How much would you have had to earn for the same period of time in 1979 to be as well off as you were in 1967? The answer is, of course, $2,170. Recall that the consumer price index in 1979 in the United States was 217 compared to 100 for the base year 1967. Stated another way, $217 in 1979 was equal to $100 in 1967 prices.

How would you convert an income of $10,000 in 1979 to 1967 prices for comparison purposes? You simply multiply the figure you wish to convert into 1967 prices by the ratio 100/217. This fraction represents the percentage change in price over the time period of 1967–1979. The numerator, 100, is the price index for the base year, 1967. The denominator, 217, is the price index for the year under consideration, 1979. The process is as follows:

$$\$10{,}000 \times \frac{100}{217} = \$4{,}600$$

Therefore, an income of $4,600 in 1967 was equivalent to an income of $10,000 in 1979.

In addition to the consumer price index, another common index used in economics is the *GNP deflator*. The GNP deflator is used to "correct" GNP figures so that they can be compared one year to the next. The term *deflator* is used since there is a tendency for GNP figures to be corrected downward year after year. In general, the value of the dollar decreases year after year rather than the other way around. The process will, however, work even if the value of the dollar increases rather than decreases. The GNP deflator for the United States for selected years from 1929 to 1979 is shown in figure 5–2.

Year	Index 1972=100	Year	Index 1972=100
1929	32.87	1955	60.98
1933	25.14	1965	74.32
1945	37.92	1978	152.09

Figure 5–2. *GNP deflator in the United States, 1929-1978 (SOURCE: Adapted from the Economic Report of the President, 1979.)*

Assume that the GNP in a base year was $1,000 billion and increased to $1,200 billion in the following year. Suppose that the GNP deflator (or price index) had changed from 100 to 105. What has happened to "real" GNP? The answer is found in the simple calculations that follow:

$$\$1{,}200 \times \frac{100}{105} = \$1{,}140$$

A GNP of $1,140 billion in the base year was equal to a GNP of $1,200 billion in the current year. The real GNP difference is $60 billion ($1,200 - $1,140) not $200 billion ($1,200 - $1,000). Stated still another way, the "current-price" GNP is $1,200 billion while the "constant" price GNP is $1,140 billion. Most charts and graphs state GNP figures in constant prices so that comparisons can be made among the various years presented. The process involved is simply that of carrying out a

The Households: Personal Economics

series of calculations so that the current-price figures are all converted to the prices for the base year. The result is then called constant-price GNP. Note, however, that you cannot compare two sets of data that have different base years. One of the sets of data would have to be converted to the base year of the other set.

The use of a price index assumes that the typical consumer will not change buying practices from year to year. This assumption holds true rather well in the short run. However, in the long run, consumers do change their buying practices quite drastically. Consequently, when you are using price indices to compare the change of prices over a long period of time, be skeptical of the figures.

Another caution that must be considered in using price indices is to note that they do not measure the change in quality of output. The quality of an automobile, for instance, might change dramatically over a twenty-year period. The price index, however, will only refer to the change in price and not the quality. Nevertheless, price indices have a great value since they do allow us to approximate "real" price changes over the years.

A knowledge of price indices is not merely of academic interest, it is of considerable practical value. For instance, labor unions, whose prime objective is to safeguard the interests of their members, pay close attention to changes in "real" income as opposed to money income. In wage negotiations between employers and labor unions, the consumer price index often forms the real basis for new wage demands. Consumer societies which are aimed at protecting the consumers also closely examine the price indices to determine whether consumers are better off or otherwise. A knowledge of the way in which money figures (both individual income figures and aggregate GNP figures) may be "corrected" to show the "real" changes are also helpful in making meaningful international comparisons of economic progress.

In the next chapter we shall analyze business firms. the I in the equation $GNP = C + I + G + F$.

six

Business Firms

In chapter 5 we discussed C by analyzing the economic role of households. In this chapter, we move to I and focus our attention upon the role of the business firm in the economy. I, of course, refers to investments which are basically handled by business firms in the economy. The topics of discussion for this chapter will include an analysis of competition, marketing practices, and business organization.

In this chapter you will find the answers to these questions:

1. What is meant by pure competition?
2. What is meant by pure monopoly?
3. What are the points in between pure competition and pure monopoly?
4. What is the significance of marketing?
5. What are the major functions of marketing?
6. What are the principal marketing channels?
7. What are the legal types of business organizations?

Pure Competition, Pure Monopoly, and the Points in Between

Business organizations produce and make available to us the economic goods and services that we need and want. *Business,* then, is the process of buying, transforming, and selling that occurs as the marketplace functions to satisfy human wants. If a business firm is to make a profit in the process of fulfilling the needs and wants of people for economic goods and services, it must deliver those goods and services in a manner that is pleasing and satisfactory to customers at a price that they consider to be fair and reasonable. In the process, businesses compete with one another for consumer patronage. *Competition* is the effort of many business firms or individuals acting independently to attract a customer. The amount of competition varies from business to business.

The three basic competitive conditions include (1) pure competition, (2) pure monopoly, and (3) imperfect competition.

Pure Competition

Economists recognize a condition of pure competition when all the following factors exist:

1. There are enough buyers and sellers so that no one buyer or seller can influence the market price.
2. All sellers market an identical product.
3. There is freedom of entry into the market by new businesses.
4. All buyers and sellers are aware of actions taken by all other buyers and sellers.
5. All buyers and sellers act rationally.

Pure competition is illustrated in figure 6–1.

Figure 6–1.

The five requirements for pure competition make it apparent that such a condition seldom, if ever, exists. However, the model of pure competition is helpful to gain a better understanding of the true nature of competition in a market economy.

Probably agriculture serves as the best approximation of pure competition. The individual farmer has virtually no control over the price of a product like wheat. And a

62   Business Firms

flour miller is basically indifferent as to whose wheat is purchased as long as the wheat from different farmers is of equal quality.

Marketing efforts under a condition of pure competition would be almost nonexistent since the seller could do little or nothing to distinguish his or her product from that of another seller. If, in fact, a seller were successful in *differentiating* (making a distinction) his or her product, pure competition, by definition, would no longer exist.

Some observers of a market-oriented economy like the United States imply that pure competition is the standard, or at least the model, for business. It seems safe to assume that these people have little knowledge of the true nature of competition. As you will see, competition can be extremely rugged without being "pure." Also it seems safe to assume that few individuals in any economy would prefer a system that produced only undifferentiated products. We want different types of automobiles, homes, and clothes to choose from.

Just as pure competition represents one market extreme, pure monopoly represents the other extreme.

Pure Monopoly

Economists recognize a condition of pure monopoly when:

1. There is a sole seller of a product or service.
2. There is no adequate substitute for the product or service.

Figure 6-2.

The two requirements for pure monopoly make it apparent that such a condition seldom, if ever, exists. The model of pure monopoly, however, like the model of pure competition, adds to our understanding of the true nature of competition within a market-oriented economy.

Probably a public utility such as a telephone company serves as the best approximation of pure monopoly. Normally, it is economically undesirable to have more than one telephone company serve a particular community and there is no really good substitute for a telephone.

The monopolist, however, seldom has the opportunity to set the market price. Government regulation of prices is severe in most monopolistic markets. In addition, the monopolist, like other business people, strives to maintain a profitable operation. As a result, many monopolistic businesses tend to be extremely efficient.

Imperfect Competition

Most businesses fall between pure competition and pure monopoly. The range between the two extremes is called *imperfect competition.*

When so few firms exist that the action of any one of the firms is noted and felt immediately by the other firms, the market condition is called an *oligopoly.*

Figure 6–3.

An oligopoly exists when the actions—e.g., price cuts, changes in product quality, sales promotion changes, or any other marketing actions—of any one "oligopolist" has an immediate effect upon the other oligopolists and brings about repercussions. For example, if General Motors cuts the price of one of its leading automobile lines, Ford and Chrysler cannot simply ignore the action. Even if Ford and Chrysler choose not to cut the prices on their competitive lines, their response not to cut prices will have its repercussions.

Actions taken by individual firms in the range known as imperfect competition are less apt to have major effects upon the other firms. And the repercussions of those actions are less dramatic. For example, one furniture dealer can change his or her marketing practices or prices without the effects or repercussions that would exist in the automobile industry.

The term *imperfect competition* should not be viewed as competition that is less desirable. Indeed, the most rugged competition that exists within developed economies is often among firms engaged in imperfect competition. The primary basis for this type of competition is the concept of *differentiation*.

The Concept of Differentiation. Assuming equal quality, a flour miller views different bushels of wheat with detached indifference. This condition is, however, the exception rather than the rule. For example, most buyers of automobiles do not view competing lines with indifference. Most potential customers are not indifferent about the firms from which they can make purchases. They may, for example, prefer to shop in a store that has a convenient location, a reputation for fair dealing, a pleasant atmosphere, and courteous employees—even if the store has slightly higher prices than some of its competitors. The point is that potential customers *differentiate* among products and among competing marketers.

The differentiation may be real or fancied; it really does not matter. What matters to the marketer is that differentiation affects sales. For example, most brands of aspirin are essentially alike; yet Bayer Aspirin enjoys a degree of differentiation in the minds of enough potential customers that it has a "partial monopoly."

Price Competition. Under pure competition, the seller cannot influence price. Under pure monopoly, the monopolist sets the most profitable price. How does price competition affect firms engaged in imperfect competition?

At first thought, you might assume that price competition would be the major form of competition in an imperfect market. Before the energy crisis of the late '70s, for example, there were major gasoline price wars. Or you may have witnessed price wars between major department stores in a given city. Macy's and Gimbel's in New York City are examples of department stores that frequently engage in price wars in their efforts to attract customers away from each other.

Price competition tends to be most prevalent among firms that are more competitive than oligopolistic. The primary reason for this condition is that the actions of any one marketer in this group of firms has limited immediate effects upon the other marketers.

However, as the market structure becomes increasingly oligopolistic, price cutting becomes a less effective device for meeting competition. In fact, the tactic might boomerang. When there are only a few sellers, and particularly when the product is not strongly differentiated (for example, steel), price cuts can set off a chain reaction that adversely affects all members of the group. Experience has taught most members of an oligopoly to "live and let live" as far as prices are concerned. This does not, however, mean that competition fails to exist.

Nonprice Competition. Product and other forms of differentiation which exist in the minds of potential customers lead to nonprice competition. For example, one customer might prefer a Ford, another a Chevrolet. Most marketing specialists have direct responsibility for this type of competition. Prices, in contrast, are normally set to correspond to cost and profit considerations. Thus, nonprice competition dominates the strategy of dynamic marketing.

Nonprice competition does not dominate in market-oriented economies because marketing specialists want it that way. Marketing comes about *in response to* the social structure.

It seems a safe assumption that many marketing executives would prefer more price competition and less nonprice competition. Price competition is more easily administered and does not have the complexities and subtlties which characterize nonprice competition.

Aside from the economic considerations already discussed, price competition is often viewed as illegal and unethical. Cutthroat pricing and other forms of price competition have frequently led to bitter legal battles. Nonprice competition has, in contrast, generally enjoyed legal sanction.

The ethical environment of nonprice competition is not so clear. Most people appear to accept the proposition that sellers should compete vigorously on nonprice terms for their patronage. However, people want such nonprice competition to take place on a high moral plane; biases, misleading advertising, or actual falsification of information by the seller are considered intolerable.

Also, the charge has been made that nonprice competition is an economic waste since funds for it could be spent for something "real." The cost of nonprice competition in the United States has been estimated to add up to as much as 10 percent of the Gross National Product.

Critics of nonprice competition state that it (1) increases costs but not total demand, (2) promotes wasteful obsolescence, (3) appeals too much to emotions, (4) controls the communication media, and (5) is often in poor taste. Proponents of nonprice competition respond that it (1) can help to stabilize the economy, (2) often makes lower prices possible through mass marketing, (3) enhances individual freedom by allowing consumers the right of "uneconomical" obsolescence, (4) frees the communication media from political control, and (5) must be in good taste to merit customer support.

Probably, the most important point to remember about nonprice competition, however, is that it is a marketing response to the social structure. Where price competition does not function effectively, competition still remains. Nonprice competition is often the most rugged, the most difficult, the most challenging, and the most creative. Thus, to compete effectively in nonprice terms, the marketer needs to thoroughly understand the market.

Marketing

Marketing is the performance of those business activities that direct the flow of goods and services from producer to consumer or user. The significance of marketing increases as an economy becomes more developed. When many goods and services are produced, potential buyers must be informed. The economic well-being of a country depends to a large extent upon marketing.

Marketing Adds Utility

As you know from chapter 1, the value that a particular product has is called its utility. There are four general types of utility:

1. *Form utility* is created by actually changing the forms of goods. For example, timber is converted into furniture and crude oil is converted into gasoline.

2. *Time utility* is created by making a product available when it is needed.
3. *Place utility* is created by making a product available where it is needed.
4. *Possession utility* is created by placing a product under the control of a person who wants it.

Marketing is concerned primarily with time, place, and possession utilities. Only those minor adjustments in form utility that are necessary on the spot to complete the transfer of a product from producer to consumer are considered to be part of marketing. For example, a retailer might adjust the length of a pair of trousers at the time of sale. In this case, that adjustment would be considered a part of marketing. The actual making of the trousers, however, is considered a part of production, not marketing. Thus, agricultural productive activities and manufacturing are not included in marketing.

Functions of Marketing

Some of the functions of marketing involve the physical handling of goods; others involve the rendering of service.

There is a tendency for some people to think that marketing functions can be eliminated. In fact, you even sometimes hear advertising that states essentially that the business firm is offering you a product for less because it has "eliminated the middleman." You should, however, be aware that the marketing functions are important and necessary if goods are to reach the consumer. The question is not one of eliminating the function; it is rather one of performing the function most efficiently.

Assembling. Assembling means accumulating or gathering goods from various sources. Wholesalers, for example, assemble goods from manufacturers or producers and distribute them to retailers. Retailers assemble goods from wholesalers.

Buying. Buying activities include (1) the agreement on prices and terms of purchase, date of shipment or delivery, and transfer of title, (2) careful determination of needs, (3) selection of sources of supply, and (4) the determination of the quality and suitability of the goods.

Storing. Storing is the process of retaining goods for varying periods of time. The demand for potatoes, for example, is fairly constant, but potato production is seasonal. Perishable foods are often stored in cold storage facilities. Many other goods require special types of storage facilities.

Standardizing. Standardizing is the process of preparing a definition or description of the various qualities of a commodity. When description of a commodity has been established, a customer can then buy the same commodity again and again with assurance that it will meet the minimum specification indicated in the description. Most products sold in cans are standardized.

Personal Selling. Personal selling is a process of direct communication between the buyer of a product and the seller. Retail salespeople, for example, engage in personal selling.

Advertising. Advertising is the indirect communication between the buyer of a product and the seller. Advertising is generally directed at a large or mass audience. Advertising is done by way of radio, television, newspapers, magazines, hand bills, signs, and many other ways.

Merchandising. Merchandising is the process of actually filling demands for products. There are basically two types of merchandising activities. The first one is that of providing the climate or setting for buying and selling to take place. Merchandising activities in this category would include the display of goods, the demonstrating of goods, and providing product and market information. The second general area of merchandising involves transferring the goods to the buyer after the sale has been made. Merchandising activities in this category involve delivery services, credit, installation, and repair services.

Transporting. Transporting is the process of getting the goods from the original producer to the ultimate consumer. Transportation involves the use of railroads, truck lines, pipelines, ships and barges, airlines, and other modes of transport.

Communication. Communicating is the process of transferring information from one person to another. Information of all sorts needs to be transferred to the marketing process. Communication can be done in person or by use of devices such as the telephone, telegraph, and postal services.

Financing. Financing is the process of providing for the money that is invested in goods while they move from one producer to the consumer. The process of moving the goods from the original producer to the consumer frequently involves long periods of time. Someone owns the goods while they move through this route. Quite often the owner of the goods does not like to keep money invested in the goods as they move through the marketing process. Consequently, the owner will obtain a loan. Other examples of financing include the sale of goods by a retailer to the consumer on credit or the extension of credit by a wholesaler to a retailer.

Risk Taking. Risk taking is the process of investing funds in a business in the hope of earning a profit. In economics, risk takers are called *entrepreneurs*. Business would not be initiated if it were not for the risk takers.

Marketing Channels

As you know, goods move on route from the producer to the ultimate consumer through various *middlemen*. A middleman is any person who performs a marketing function. The course the goods take is called the *marketing channel*. The *manufacturer* is the individual or business firm who processes the product. A *wholesaler* buys products from various manufacturers and, in turn, distributes these products to retailers. Retailers sell products directly to the ultimate consumer. Various types of agents operate throughout the marketing process. An *agent* is simply any person who acts for another person in the buying or selling of a product. When a buyer or seller cannot deal directly, she or he will frequently employ the services of an agent. The most common marketing channels are illustrated in figure 6-4.

68   Business Firms

Figure 6-4. *The major marketing channels.*

Legal Forms of Private Business Enterprise

The four principal types of business organizations under private enterprise include (1) the sole proprietorship, (2) the partnership, (3) corporations, and (4) cooperatives.

The legal form of a business will affect the laws under which it operates, the liability of the owners for debts incurred in the business enterprise, the taxes that will need to be paid, the role of management, and business financing.

Sole Proprietorship

A *sole proprietorship* is one that is owned and managed by one person. This is the oldest and simplest form of business organization in existence today.

Anyone who has the desire, ability, ambition, and necessary money capital can start a business as a sole proprietor. Naturally this person must follow all legal and license requirements. The business is the owner's personal property. The income from the business is taxed as personal income and the business debts are also considered as personal debts. When personal wealth can be demanded in payment of business debts, the situation is called *unlimited liability*. A sole proprietor has unlimited liability for the debts of his or her business.

The main advantage of the sole proprietorship is that it is easy to start, and the sole proprietor has basically unlimited freedom to run the business as he or she sees fit as long as the laws and regulations applicable to the business are followed. If the business is successful, the owner does not have to share the profit with anyone after the taxes are paid. There is also an advantage on the payment of taxes since the income of a sole proprietorship is free from "double taxation." The earnings of most corporations—there are some exceptions—are taxed before dividends are distributed; the person who receives the dividend (one of the owners of the company) must then pay a personal income tax on the dividend. This is what is meant by double taxation.

The sole proprietor may have difficulty raising money capital to buy the tools, machinery, factory buildings, office buildings, and other types of capital needed in the business. Since the sole proprietorship lasts no longer than the active life of the proprietor, creditors do not want to lend large sums for long periods. Additionally, since the business is owned and operated by one person, there is a greater risk to the creditor in the event that anything would happen to the sole proprietor. Also, it is more difficult for one person to be able to adequately secure (back up) the loan with personal wealth in the event that the business does not work out well.

Most small businesses are sole proprietorships. Consequently, there are more sole proprietorships in existence than any other form of business organization. However, very few large businesses use this form of business organization because of the difficulty of raising money capital and the limited life of the business. Consequently, most of the total volume of business conducted in the United States is in organizations other than a sole proprietorship.

Partnership

A *partnership* is a business that is owned and managed by two or more individuals. The partnership agreement (a contract) is often explicitly stated in writing but does not have to be so stated to be legally binding. The agreement usually specifies such things as how much each partner will contribute and what percentage of the earnings will go to each partner. The earnings are taxed as personal income. Generally each partner is liable for all contracts *in connection with the business* that are made by any other partner, and each partner is liable to the full extent of his or her personal property. This is called *joint and several liability* and is one reason why partners are chosen with such care.

However, it is possible in writing a partnership agreement to provide for *limited partners*. Under such an agreement, called a *limited partnership*, the general partners have unlimited liability but the limited partners have limited liability. The limited partners are usually also *silent partners*. This term is used to designate that these partners do not have an active voice in the management of the partnership but share a percentage of the profit (or losses).

If a partner dies or leaves the firm, the partnership is automatically dissolved. The business may be formed again, but it will be a new or different partnership.

A partnership has the advantage that it combines the special talents of two or more partners. In addition, it is easier for two or more people to raise the money capital needed than it is for a sole proprietor. Naturally, a limitation of the partnership is the fact that there is less freedom in business judgment than in the case of a sole proprietorship and business profits must be shared when the business is successful.

The Corporation

The *corporation*, or *joint-stock company* as it is called in some countries, is without a doubt the most important form of business organization for a large-scale business enterprise in the world today. A corporation is owned by *stockholders*, each owning one or more *shares of stock*. The shareholders are the real owners of the business. The shareholders, however, select a *board of directors* to set the general policy for the company. The directors usually delegate much of the responsibility for the management of the business to officers and career management people. Sometimes the officers of the company also serve as members of the board of directors. Generally, the officers of a corporation include the president, a vice president, the secretary, and the treasurer. The organization of a corporation is illustrated in figure 6–5.

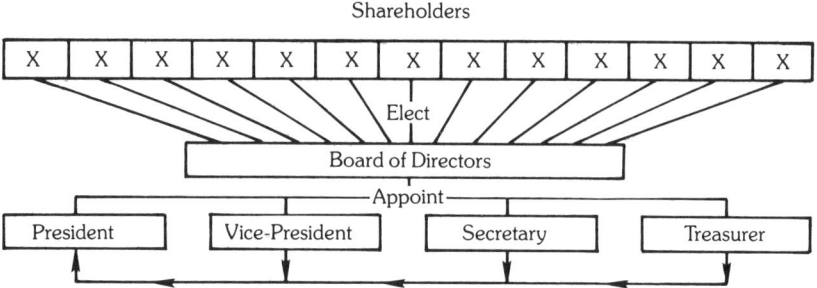

Figure 6-5. *Chart of the organization of a corporation.*

The major feature of a corporation is that it provides for *limited liability*. Each shareholder is liable only for the amount of money he or she has invested in the shares. A shareholder does not risk his or her private wealth.

To form a corporation, a group of people obtain a state charter. The charter sets forth the name of the company, the place where it will do business, the objectives of the company, the procedure for the issuing of stock, and the liability of different classes of stockholders.

The purpose and functions of the business are stated in more detail in a document called the *articles of incorporation*. This document details such items as the purpose of the company, rules for electing the directors, names of the principal owners, how much stock the company can issue, and how long the life of the company will be.

A corporation is a handy tool for raising large amounts of money capital since many people can buy stock. Each share represents an equal part of the ownership of the company.

If a company earns a profit, it may distribute part of the profit to its owners (the shareholders) by way of dividends. The dividends are distributed by paying equal amounts for identical shares of stock. Thus, each stockholder receives payment according to the number of shares he or she owns.

The directors do not have to declare dividends even if profits are earned. In most countries, dividends are not a legal obligation that must be paid such as the interest on debts. However, since directors are elected by the shareholders, they usually pay dividends whenever possible—sometimes even in years when losses are sustained.

Corporations are classified as being either private or public.

A Private Corporation. Since private corporations do not offer their securities to the general public, the company need not make its investment business activities known to the general public.

Many family-held large businesses are private corporations. It provides an opportunity for a family to retain control of its investments and at the same time enjoy limited liability.

A Public Corporation. A public corporation is one that offers its stock for general sale to anyone who wishes to buy it. The securities of a public corporation are generally of the following types:

1. Common Stock. The shareholders who own common stock are the personal risk takers of the business since they own the equity capital. They receive any profits that the business earns after all other forms of creditors and investors are paid. Consequently, they take a bigger risk, but they also have the possibility of sharing a greater return.

2. Preferred Stock. The shareholders who hold preferred stock are paid a dividend out of profits before anything is paid to the common stockholders. The rate of return for preferred shares of stock is set at a fixed percentage.

It is possible for preferred stock to be convertible. When it is convertible, it means that preferred stock can be traded for common stock, either at a specified price per share or on the basis of so many shares of preferred stock for so many shares of common stock. This privilege has an advantage if the common stock increases in value. The preferred stockholder does not take as great of a risk as the common stockholder. In economics, however, the preferred stockholder is generally classified as an entrepreneur since the return is in the form of a dividend that is paid from profits.

3. Bonds. Bonds are evidence of a debt owed by a company; they do not represent a share of an ownership of the enterprise. When a business issues bonds, it acknowledges that it owes the holders a certain sum of money and agrees to repay the sum on a certain date and under certain conditions. The business also agrees to pay interest at a specified rate and at specified intervals. The holder of the business bond is not generally considered to be an entrepreneur since she or he receives interest whether or not the business makes a profit.

Cooperatives

A *cooperative* is a form of business organization in which individuals become members usually by depositing a nominal sum of money or purchasing a share of stock. The membership of a cooperative mainly consists of individuals with a common interest. For example, the producers of a certain farm product such as livestock might join together to form a *producers* cooperative. Other types of cooperatives are sometimes organized for special groups of consumers. For example, the employees of a certain manufacturing firm or a government agency might band together in a cooperative society. An extremely common form of cooperative of this type is a *credit union*. The purpose of the credit union is to provide loans to its members at a relatively low cost with limited security and at the same time provide a fairly high rate of return for people who invest money in the credit union.

The death or withdrawal of a member does not affect the length of life of a cooperative. Cooperatives operate on the principle that goods and services will be provided to members at cost. Therefore, there is no legal profit in a cooperative. Any accumulation of funds that results from the operation of the business is returned to members as *patronage dividends*. Consequently, a cooperative does not pay federal income taxes.

The owners and managers of corporations often argue that cooperatives have an unfair advantage because they are exempt from federal income taxes. A corporation pays taxes on its income before dividends are distributed to the stockholders. The stockholders in turn pay taxes on the dividends they receive. Consequently, there is *double taxation*. In a cooperative, there are no legal profits. Consequently, the cooperative does not pay federal income taxes. The only taxes that are paid are by the stockholders when they receive their patronage dividends. A cooperative is free from double taxation.

The major advantage of a cooperative is that savings that are possible through collective action can be shared with the membership. A primary disadvantage of a cooperative is that the member, in order to reap the reward from membership, must do business with the cooperative. Patronage dividends are distributed on the basis of the amount of business done with the cooperative. A common problem experienced by cooperatives is maintaining a skilled management staff. Quite frequently, corporations put a higher premium on a skilled management staff than do cooperatives. Cooperatives generally pay lower salaries to their managers. As a result, cooperatives either (1) attract a lower quality management staff or (2) run the risk of having qualified managers attracted away by corporations through higher salary offerings.

Financing a Corporation

A large corporation needs a good deal of money capital to get started and to maintain its business operation. The four basic sources of money capital for a corporation include (1) the sale of securities, (2) bank loans, (3) insurance company loans, and (4) book credit.

Sale of Securities. The word *securities* refers to all of the stocks and bonds issued by a company. The stocks, of course, represent ownership. Bond holders are creditors of the business. Stockholders receive dividends and bond holders receive interest.

The money originally invested by stockholders in a company is called *equity capital*. This simply means that these stockholders have an equity in the business and have provided for the capital that the business will use. The business uses the money of the stockholders to buy buildings, machines, tools, and the like. The stockholders are willing to invest in the business in the hope of participating in the profits. When a business firm raises money in this way, it usually enters into a contract with a person or business that specializes in the sale of equity capital stocks with bonds. This type of individual or firm is usually called an *underwriter*. The underwriter buys the entire block of stocks and bonds from the company at a price lower than the expected resale price. The company then receives its money in one transaction rather than having to solicit the sale of a number of potential stockholders. The underwriter, in turn, receives profits from selling the shares of stock at a price slightly higher than the original purchase price.

It is only at the time that the shares of stock are originally issued and sold that the corporation receives any money from the sale of securities. Once the underwriter has sold the securities to the general public, the future sale of these securities does not affect the finance of the corporation directly. For example, if Mr. A owns a share of common stock in the XYZ Company, and he sells this share to Ms. B the transaction does not involve XYZ financially.

There are two types of markets in which stocks and bonds are easily bought and sold. The first market is a *stock exchange*. A stock exchange is merely a location where securities are bought and sold by means of the auction method. A security is offered for sale at a certain price or someone may bid for the same security at a different price. A sale takes place when someone buys the security at the price offered. These offers (sometimes called asking prices) and bids go on regularly and often at a rapid pace. Therefore, anyone who owns a security that is traded on a stock exchange has a fairly good idea of the price that the security can be sold for at any given time.

The other main market for securities is what is called the over-the-counter market. Securities that are not traded at stock exchanges are bought and sold through individual brokers. The transactions are called over-the-counter transactions. Securities sold in this manner may be equally as good as securities sold on a stock exchange but they are not as easily bought or sold.

Bank Loans. Corporations frequently obtain loans from commercial banks. These loans are used to purchase the capital needed by the business. The amount of money that a bank will loan to a business depends on the amount of money that stockholders have already invested in the business and the business prospects for profit.

Insurance Company Loans. Insurance companies have large sums of money that they receive from their policyholders. Most insurance policies do not mature for a long period of time. Therefore, the insurance company has money from the policyholders to invest before the funds are returned to the policyholders in the form of insurance payments. Frequently, insurance companies will make loans to corporations. In fact, loans from insurance companies are a major source of financing for corporations. The reason for this is that insurance companies are frequently able to give larger loans than a bank.

Book Credit. Most businesses engage in the use of book credit. This simply means that buyers are allowed a certain special period of time (usually thirty days or more) to pay for the goods they have purchased. The use of book credit by a business is similar to the use of credit cards by an individual. Book credit does constitute a form of loan when used by a business.

In the next chapter we shall analyze government, the G in the equation $GNP = C + I + G + F$.

seven

Government: Spending and Taxing

As you know from our previous discussion, the government can act either as a consumer or as an investor. In the equation, GNP $= C + I + G + F$, the spending done by government is separated for accounting purposes. Stated another way, the G in the equation combines elements of both C and I. In the last chapter, you examined how government influences business investment, I. In this chapter you will have an opportunity to examine the entire range of government spending, G. You will also have an opportunity to examine public policies as they relate to government spending.

In this chapter you will find the answers to these questions:

1. Where do government dollars go?
2. Where do government dollars come from?
3. What is meant by fiscal policy?
4. How does fiscal policy affect the economy?

Federal Government Spending

The government buys goods and services in an attempt to promote the general welfare of the nation. Basically, in a market-oriented economy, the government will

Government: Spending and Taxing

supply only those goods and services that are not easily produced in the private sector. Goods and services which the community or society as a whole needs and which are best satisfied on a group basis are called "collective wants." For example, the government will provide for national defense against an external attack and for the internal security of the nation. These services accrue to all individuals in the country and are provided through the government. It would be literally impossible for an individual to purchase an item such as defense for himself or herself. Although an individual could purchase police protection on an individual basis, the cost would be exorbitant and the system unduly cumbersome. Likewise, a system of private education could be established, but a public educational system extends education privileges and benefits to the entire nation.

Figure 7–1 illustrates changes in the federal budget from 1960 to 1980 (estimated).

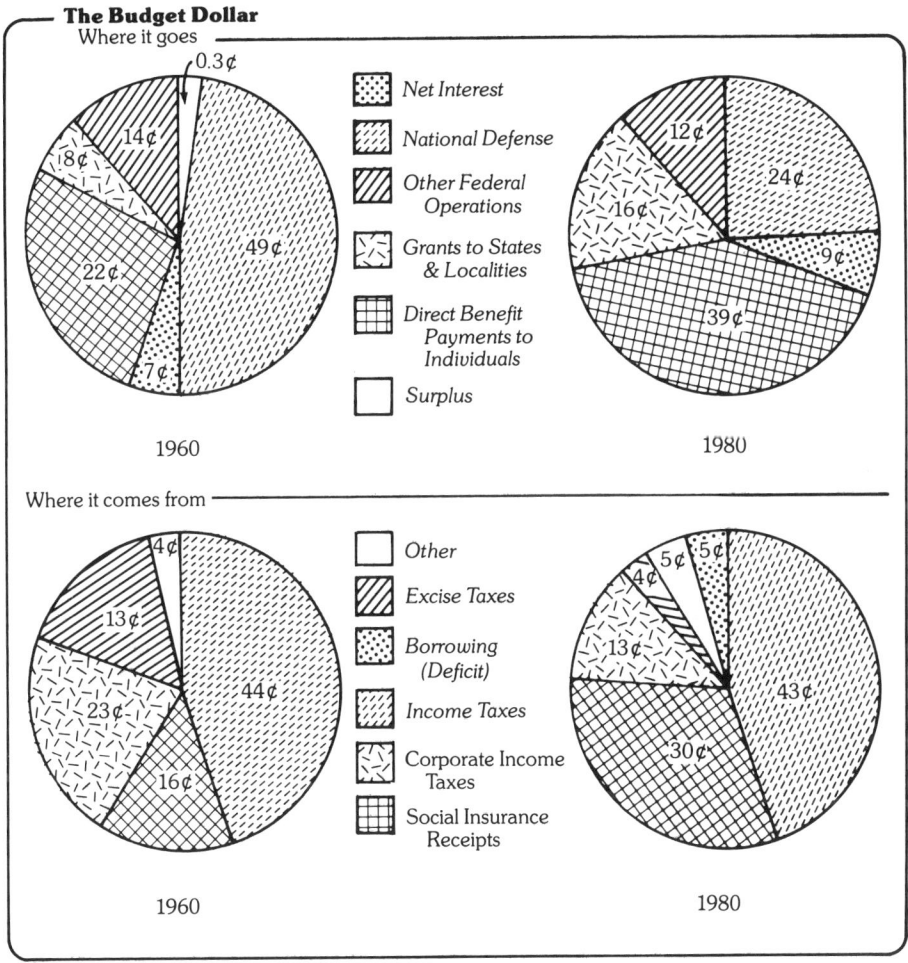

Figure 7–1. *The federal budget.*

Federal Government Taxing

The federal government receives most of its income through taxes. The two basic principles of taxing policy include (1) the benefit principle, and (2) the ability to pay principle.

The *benefit principle* merely states that those people or businesses that benefit from the government service should pay the tax. An entrance fee at a government park is an example of the use of the benefit principle. Those who use the park pay for its upkeep by virtue of the entrance fee. A tax on gasoline is another attempt at relating the service provided to its cost. In this case, those who use the roads more pay more for road repair and upkeep.

Even if it were desirable to do so, not all government goods and services can be priced according to who receives the greatest benefit from these services. For example, how would the benefits of a government purchase of a new military tank be allocated among the citizens. Generally, expenditures of this type are shared according to an ability to pay principle.

The *ability to pay principle* merely states that people or businesses that have the most income or wealth should pay the most in taxes.

The basic argument behind the ability to pay principle is that people who have more income or wealth do not face as great a burden in the payment of their taxes as those with lower income. Also the ability to pay principle is very closely related to the benefit principle since people with greater income and wealth have more to lose if the government does not maintain its economic, social, and military strength.

The basic three types of tax schemes are (1) progressive, (2) proportional, and (3) regressive. The ability to pay theory supports the notion of a progressive tax system. Under a *progressive tax system*, the percentage that a person or business pays in tax increases as the income increases. For example, a person with a low income would pay a small percentage in taxes. A person with a higher income would pay a larger percentage of his or her income in taxes.

Under a *proportional system* of taxation, the percentage of tax stays the same as a person's income increases. For example, all people might pay 30 percent of their total income in taxes. The dollar amount paid would, of course, be higher for people with higher incomes.

In a *regressive system* of taxation, the percentage of tax paid increases as a person's or business firm's income decreases. Stated another way, a person or business firm with a low income would pay a higher percentage of this income than a person or business firm with a larger income. A sales tax on basic food stuffs would be an example of a regressive tax since poor people spend a greater percentage of their total income on food than richer people do.

The equation $GNP = C + I + G + F$ indicates the sources for government revenue. Income to the government must be provided through one or more of the following three sources: consumer (C), businesses (I), and foreign trade (F). Consequently, taxes can be classified as (1) household taxes, (2) business taxes, and (3) export-import taxes.

Household taxes can be further categorized into (1) taxes on personal income, (2) taxes on real estate properties, (3) social security taxes, and (4) death and gift taxes.

Business taxes can be categorized into (1) taxes on nonchartered businesses, such as sole proprietorship and partnerships, (2) taxes imposed on the profits of corporations, (3) employment (payroll) taxes paid by employers, (4) sales taxes imposed on the purchase of certain items at the time of sale, (5) excise taxes, which are essentially the same as the sales tax but are imposed on items that are considered to be luxuries rather than necessities, and (6) taxes imposed on real estate owned by business.

Import-export taxes can be categorized into (1) import duties and (2) export duties.

The sources of revenue for the United States federal government in 1960 and 1980 (estimated) are presented in figure 7–1.

Note that the projected U.S. government tax receipts for 1980 are less than the projected expenditures, leaving a deficit. Deficit financing is not unusual in most countries today. In the United States, the federal government has run a deficit about two out of every three years since World War II. The gross federal debt at the end of 1978 was $782 billion. Deficits and debt financing often lead to problems of inflation and unemployment.

The Phillips Curve

Generally, there is a "trade off" between unemployment and inflation. The more unemployment that an economy is willing to tolerate, the less inflation it will have and vice versa. The relationship between unemployment and inflation is illustrated in figure 7–2, commonly called the *Phillips Curve* after the English economist A.W. Phillips who first noted this relationship.

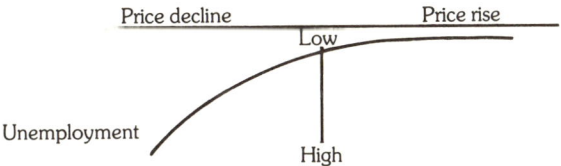

Figure 7–2. *Phillips Curve.*

You should note from figure 7–2 that the curve is generalized and does not show the exact percentage of trade-off between unemployment and inflation. The actual percentage of the trade-off will vary from country to country and from one time period to another.

One reason for a trade-off between unemployment and inflation is that a fully-employed economy tends to be overheated. You are already familiar with the situation from previous circular flow analysis. At a time that all the factors of production are fully employed, any increase in an aggregate demand simply drives prices up and causes inflation. However, when a great deal of unemployment exists an increase in aggregate demand simply pulls these idle workers into the work force.

You should note also that as an economy reaches full or acceptable employment, the workers drawn into the labor force tend to be less efficient than those previously employed. Also, at a time when unemployment increases, there is a tendency for the less efficient workers to be discharged first. Less efficient workers do not produce as much per person as efficient workers and, therefore, have a tendency to drive costs higher and in times of full employment this would mean higher prices. This situation is also reflected in the Phillips Curve.

The Phillips Curve is, as mentioned earlier, a generalized explanation of the relationship between unemployment and inflation. There are many countries where the relationship between unemployment and inflation is not as it is predicted by the Phillips Curve. In many developed and developing countries there has been a high rate of inflation together with a high rate of unemployment in recent years.

Some Fiscal Tools

The basic purposes of fiscal (federal government taxing and spending) policy are to (1) promote rapid economic growth, (2) maintain price stability, (3) minimize unemployment and underemployment, and (4) to maintain a favorable balance of trade over time.

A review of the circular flow diagram illustrates the basic fiscal policies available to the government.

Note that during a period of relatively high unemployment the government will try to take those actions which will expand the flow of goods and services (and money). Stated differently, the government will try to increase the flow of labor from the household to the firm. This action will, in turn, increase the income payments that go from the firm to the household. During an inflationary period the government's action would be just the reverse.

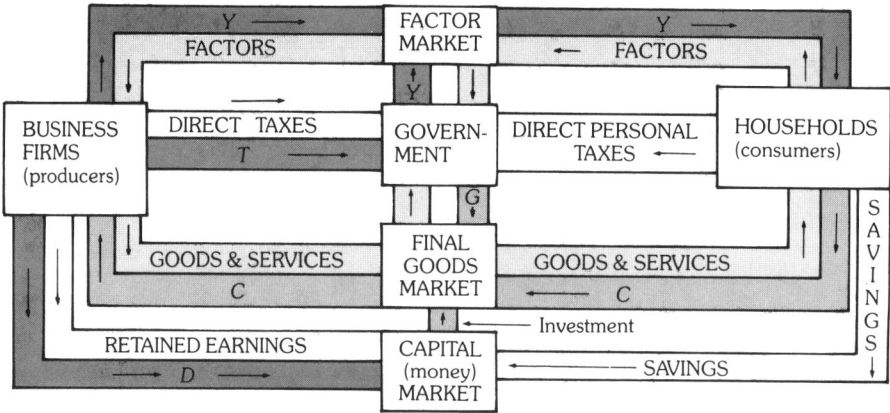

Figure 7-3. *The circular flow revisited.*

Even if the government takes no action to counter the prevailing economic situation during either a deflationary or inflationary period, certain automatic or built-in stabilizers are constantly at work which help to maintain economic stability.

The principal built-in stabilizers are as follows:

1. An automatic change in tax receipts comes about at times of inflation or recession. For example, tax revenues are increased when prices and incomes increase. This is true since (a) the higher income levels generate additional taxes and (b) the income levels are taxed at a higher rate under a progressive income tax schedule.

As you know from our discussion in chapter 4, increased taxes at a time of inflation might be needed to drain off surplus funds from the economy. This approach will decrease the income payments flowing to consumers, which, in turn, will decrease the consumer expenditure flowing from the households to business firms. The decrease in spending alleviates the inflation. A government surplus is helpful during a time of inflation. The tax system in use in most countries serves as a built-in stabilizer against instability.

At a time of deflation, the amount of taxes going to the government decreases. This means that consumers have a higher percentage of their money income to spend for consumer expenditures. Also during a deflationary period, the government might choose to operate a deficit to inject additional funds into the economy. You can trace the effects to deficit financing on the circular flow in figure 7–3.

2. Most nations operate a general system of unemployment compensation and some form of welfare payments. At a time of recession or depression, the government pumps additional money into the economy through an increase in its unemployment compensation and welfare payments. These payments increase the money flowing to the households and make it possible for households to increase their consumer expenditures which flow to the business firm. Remember also that when the household increases its consumer expenditures a multiplier effect is set into action.

3. During an inflationary period, individuals and businesses tend to save more of their funds. This is true because there is always a time gap before the individual household or business firm adjusts to the increased income. During that period of adjustment there is a tendency to increase savings. As you know, an increase in savings has a depressing effect on the economy and is exactly the type of action that is needed during an inflationary period. The reverse situation is also true during a recession, at a time a household or business firm experiences a reduction in income, there is a tendency to reduce savings and thereby provide an injection into the economic system.

The New Economics

The term *the new economics* was introduced in the early 1960s in the United States by the Kennedy administration. Today the term is rather commonly used on a worldwide basis and refers to fiscal policies that have come into being in recent years. Some of the more common types of "new economic" policies are described below.

Gap Closing and Growth. Modern economic fiscal policy is no longer aimed at merely smoothing out the ups and downs of the business cycle; rather, it is designed to create an ever-increasing rate of growth. Therefore, fiscal policy begins with a careful estimate of the trend rate of growth. This is done simply by adding together the growth rate in labor inputs and productivity. Once all of the growth rates are calculated, an average growth rate potential can be established for the nation. At that point the unemployment target is used to establish what the total GNP of a country would be at a given rate of unemployment coupled with a known potential rate of growth. In this way, the potential "real" GNP is established. If the *actual GNP* is below the *potential GNP,* then policies are taken to *close the gap.* If the actual GNP is higher than the potential real GNP, this indicates that inflation exists and steps are taken to reduce the gap back to the potential real GNP.

Fiscal Drag. A country with a progressive income tax system and a positive growth rate has a built-in increase in federal revenue each year. If this increase in revenue by the federal government is not injected into the money flow it becomes a *fiscal drag* that functions as a leakage in the money flow and chokes off economic expansion.

Fiscal Dividends. To reduce the possible harmful effects of fiscal drag, a system of *fiscal dividends* is considered as a part of modern fiscal policy. You should note, of course, that fiscal drag is helpful during an inflationary period. However, during a deflationary period, fiscal drag retards economic growth. Therefore, the government should, in terms of modern fiscal policy, declare fiscal dividends of the right size and timing to promote economic stability. For example, if a recession threatens, the declaration of a fiscal dividend would be in order. The fiscal dividends can be in the form of tax relief or grants to state governments.

Full Employment (or High Employment) Budget Surpluses (or Deficits). The procedure here is much the same as indicated previously under gap closing. The first step is to determine the potential real GNP. If the actual GNP is below the potential real GNP, then the government might choose to operate at a *planned deficit* sufficient to close the gap. If the actual GNP is inflated and therefore beyond the potential real GNP, the government might choose to operate at a surplus.

The term *full employment budget surplus* gets its name from the fact that the GNP is determined at *full employment.* The surplus refers to the excess in receipts over expenditures if the economy were operating at full capacity. Full employment is generally defined to be synonymous with the officially accepted rate of unemployment—for example, 4–5 percent. The term *surplus* should be changed to *deficit* at a time when prudent fiscal policy calls for a deficit instead of the surplus.

Under this theory, a budget surplus or a budget deficit is neither good nor bad; it is simply a tool that is used for insuring stability and growth. In a given year, to know whether a deficit or a surplus is "acceptable" you simply compare the potential real GNP with the actual GNP. If the actual GNP is less than the potential real GNP, the government might choose to operate at a deficit sufficient to close the gap. If the actual GNP is inflated and higher than the potential real GNP, the government might choose to maintain a surplus sufficient to close the gap.

Wage-Price Guideposts. The idea behind wage-price guideposts is to establish guidelines for labor-management negotiations. The principle involved is that the general wage increases should not be greater than the increase in productivity. As you know from our previous discussion, an increase in wages greater than productivity leads to inflation.

Wage-Price Freeze. The wage-price freeze is simply an involuntary control over wages and prices. Whereas wage-price guidelines are suggestive and voluntary, a wage-price freeze is not. A wage-price freeze is established at a time when the voluntary system does not appear to be functioning sufficiently well.

The Monetary "Twist." The monetary twist refers to a series of policies designed to hold down the cost of long-term funds for investments and at the same time increase short-term interest rates. The idea behind the monetary twist is to encourage individuals to save domestically rather than to send money abroad in the hope for higher rates of return. The process by which this can be done will become clear after we examine monetary policy. At this point it is only necessary for you to note that the monetary twist is one of the fiscal tools available under the new economic policies.

Some Fiscal Myths

Nearly everyone considers himself or herself to be a financial expert. In fact, knowledge about fiscal policy was slow in coming. The principles of fiscal policy really came into being on a worldwide basis during the 1930s. Sophistication in the use of fiscal tools has advanced rapidly since that time. However, many of the old myths about fiscal matters still exist. Among the many myths are:

1. The federal government must balance its budget every year, or at least every few years.
2. A public debt is a burden that will have to be borne by our children and grandchildren.
3. An individual should not go into debt; neither should the government.
4. If a government goes into debt, it will go into bankruptcy. The same goes for an individual who goes too far into debt.
5. A good tax is one that will produce the same revenue in good times as in bad times.
6. The best way to get out of a depression or a recession is to tighten up the government purse strings and spend less public money.

Some of these myths were explored briefly in this chapter; the others will be considered elsewhere in this textbook—mainly in chapter 9. In the next chapter we shall analyze foreign trade, the F in the equation $GNP = C + I + G + F$.

eight

International Trade

There is a tendency in the United States to take limited notice of the significance of international trade. After all, international trade (F in the formula GNP $= C + I + G + F$) represents only about 5 percent of our GNP. For that reason many Americans feel that the United States is relatively self-sufficient and could survive without foreign trade.

Citizens of other nations generally accept the importance of foreign trade without question. In a developing nation, up to 50 percent of the GNP might be exported. More than 20 percent of the national income of such well developed countries as Canada and England is derived from international trade. Japan has basically built its dynamic economic growth since World War II on trade with other countries.

But what about the United States? The energy crunch of the 1970s showed dramatically how dependent Americans are on world markets.

Many strategic metals are virtually nonexistent in the United States, e.g., bauxite, manganese, cobalt, nickel, tin, platinum, and asbestos. Americans also import a large amount of raw materials such as copper, iron ore, and timber. Many foodstuffs are also purchased abroad, e.g., coffee, tea, rice, pepper, and bananas.

International specialization and the trade that is developed from it has made the world economy extremely interdependent. A breakdown in foreign trade would be very much like the breaking of a link in a chain. Also the economic problems in one country have a tendency to be "exported" to other countries. Inflation is seldom, for example, confined within the borders of one country. Although foreign trade is similar in many ways to domestic trade, certain problems and characteristics arise that deserve special attention.

In this chapter you will find the answers to these questions:

1. What are the advantages of international or foreign trade?
2. What are the characteristics of international or foreign trade?
3. How does foreign trade fit into the circular flow of goods and services?

Advantages of Foreign Trade

A furniture dealer in Grand Rapids, Michigan, likes to have steak available for backyard cookouts. An operator of a feeding lot in Greeley, Colorado, enjoys the comfort of furniture assembled in Grand Rapids. The two individuals involved need not meet directly to negotiate a trade of beef for furniture. Nonetheless, a trade can indeed take place, and both people are better off because of the transaction. The businessperson in Grand Rapids specializes in the assembly of furniture. The feed lot operator in Greeley specializes in producing beef. If the businessperson in Grand Rapids were to produce beef and the feed lot operator in Greeley were to attempt to assemble furniture, neither would live as well as each does with trade. Transactions of this type are common and you see the results of them everyday. As you know from previous chapters, people live better because of specialization.

For some reason, once trade extends beyond the boundaries of the nation, simple logic and the easily understood advantages of trade are often confused. For example, it is not uncommon to hear such statements as "When there is a trade transaction between two nations, one nation benefits more than the other." Or, you might have heard a statement such as the following. "Developed countries cannot compete with underdeveloped countries because of the cheaper labor in the underdeveloped nations."

Are statements like these actually true? The basis for trade between and among nations is really the same as the basis for trade within nations. However, the situation is often complicated because of interference in the normal trade flow. One reason for such interference is that most countries like to be as self-sufficient as possible.

Trade among nations promotes a sharing of cultural traditions, helps people to understand each other better, promotes the basis for international friendships, and allows for and permits both countries to live better by specializing in the production of certain goods and services.

When viewed from the point of view of the individual businessperson, each manufacturer or distributor wants to have an opportunity to export goods and services to other countries. These exports expand the market and make it possible for a businessperson to increase business activity and thus enhance the chance to make a greater profit.

Absolute Advantage

A basis for engaging in international trade may be illustrated by the following situation. Assume a situation in which (a) free trade (no duties or tariffs) exists between the nations, (b) products produced by one country are equal to the products produced in the other country, (c) there are no transportation costs, and (d) there is no national prejudice between the nations involved. Further assume that costs to produce are as shown in chart 8–1.

Chart 8 – 1.

Product	Nation A Cost to Produce	Nation B Cost to Produce
Bicycle	$20.00	$19.00
Roller skates	2.00	2.50

The manufacturer of the bicycle in Nation B can compete favorably for export business with Nation A. Manufacturers of bicycles in Nation A will either find a way of reducing cost to produce a bicycle, or they may be forced to shift to another product if they wish to engage in international trade.

The situation is just reversed in the case of the roller skates. Manufacturers in Nation A can compete favorably with manufactuers of roller skates in Nation B. Manufacturers of roller skates in Nation B will have to find a way to reduce the cost to produce roller skates or shift to some other product.

Nation A has an *absolute advantage* over Nation B in producing roller skates. Nation B has an absolute advantage over Nation A in producing bicycles. What would happen, we might ask, if one of the nations had an absolute advantage in producing bicycles and roller skates? Would trade be profitable for either or both countries? The answer is yes, and both countries would benefit from international trade. The answer is found in what economists call *comparative advantage.*

Comparative Advantage

Assume a trade example whereby Nation A has an absolute advantage in the production of both bicycles and roller skates (see chart 8–2).

Chart 8–2.

Product	Nation A Cost to Produce	Nation B Cost to Produce
Bicycle	$20.00	$30.00
Roller Skates	2.00	5.00

In Nation A, without trade with Nation B, a bicycle is worth ten pairs of roller skates. In Nation B, without trade with Nation A, a bicycle is worth six pairs of roller skates.

Now, assuming that the two nations are free to trade without duties or tariffs, what happens? If Nation A produces only roller skates, it can, for instance, produce thirty pairs for $60. Since a bicycle in Nation B costs six pairs of roller skates, Nation A can use, say, twelve pairs of skates to buy two bicycles from Nation B. Now Nation A has two bicycles and eighteen pairs of skates for a cost of $60. Without trade, eighteen pairs of skates would have cost $36 and the two bicycles would have cost $40 for a total expenditure of $76.

If Nation B produces only bicycles, it can produce two for $60. If it trades one of these bicycles to Nation A, it can get ten pairs of roller skates. Therefore, for a cost of $60 Nation B has one bicycle and ten pairs of roller skates. Without trade, ten pairs of roller skates in Nation B would have cost $50 and a bicycle would have cost $30 for a total expenditure of $80.

Both nations are better off because of trade even though Nation A has an absolute advantage in producing both bicycles and roller skates. Nation A can still get more goods with a given expenditure of money, but both nations are better off. The reason, of course, is that the relative advantage in producing bicycles and roller skates is different in the two nations. Nation A is 50 percent better at producing bicycles than Nation B, but it is 150 percent better than Nation B at producing roller skates.

When each nation produces those goods and services that it can produce most efficiently and trades freely with other nations, the level of living in each country rises.

A simple example from daily experience might help to highlight the principle of comparative advantage. Suppose that an artist can earn $50 for painting a picture. It takes him or her the same time to do one picture as it takes to mow the lawn. He or she can hire the lawn mowed for $10. Even if the artist were more skilled at mowing the lawn than the person he or she hires and could do it at a cost of, say $5, would it be profitable for the artist to take painting time to mow the lawn? Would it be profitable for a skilled surgeon who is an excellent typist to take time from his or her medical practice to do his or her own typing? Might not the surgeon be better off to hire a secretary?

Stated simply, the principle of comparative advantage states that trade is mutually profitable for two nations if each specializes in the production of products in which it has the greatest relative efficiency even if one nation is absolutely more efficient in the production of every product produced.

International Dumping: A Special Case

A significant aspect of international trade that makes it different from domestic trade is what is frequently called "dumping." Through the process of dumping, certain products might well sell abroad at a price lower than they sell in the domestic market. You might wonder how this situation could be possible. Dumping comes about when an economy is not operating at full capacity—it has unused labor resources, plant facilities, and other productive capacities. In order to use these capacities to a fuller extent, the "excess" products are sold in other countries at a price less than they are made available domestically. Such a practice makes it possible for a business firm to use its full productive facilities. Consequently, it is often to the advantage of a business to dump its excess products on a foreign market. International dumping is a hindrance to foreign trade, and most governments have taken retaliatory action when the process has been disclosed.

Characteristics of International or Foreign Trade

One of the major differences between domestic trade and foreign trade is the manner in which international payments are settled. A businessperson in the United States wants to receive dollars when selling a product in Japan. The Japanese businessperson, in turn, has Japanese yen available but not dollars. Somehow the Japanese buyer must be able to obtain dollars if he or she is to buy goods or services from a seller in the United States.

The need for settling international accounts has led to what is commonly called the "Foreign Exchange Market." Actually there is no single market for foreign exchange. The principal dealers are banks that are located in the major financial centers of the world such as New York, San Francisco, London, Paris, and Tokyo. When a U.S. businessperson needs Japanese yen, he or she pays U.S. bank dollars, and the bank gives him or her a claim on yen that the bank maintains (directly or indirectly) in a bank in Japan. The bank has sold yen for dollars. In a like manner, when a Japanese importer needs dollars he or she will go to a bank in Japan and "buy" dollars for yen. If the amount of the two transactions were exactly equal, the balances in the banks of the two countries involved would cancel each other. In practical situations, however, one country has a surplus of the other country's money, and the other country has a deficit.

The supply of another country's currency results from exports. For example, when a Japanese manufacturer wishes to purchase goods in the United States, he or she must first buy U.S. dollars in Japan. The Japanese bank, in turn, has purchased the dollars from a bank in the United States by buying these dollars for yen. Consequently, the supply of yen in the United States is increased through U.S. exports to Japan. The reverse situation is true when a U.S. citizen buys a Japanese television set or tape recorder.

In the long run, the amount of exports and imports must be approximately equal, or one country or the other will build up an excess supply of foreign currency. When this happens, the supply exceeds the demand and the value of the foreign currency held decreases.

Until the mid 1970s countries adjusted foreign exchange rates (set new values) when surpluses and deficits developed. Since that time, the general practice has been to allow exchange rates to "float" to adjust automatically to supply and demand conditions.

Entrepot Trade

Some ports, such as Singapore, Hong Kong, and Penang, do a good deal of business essentially operating as middlemen for goods produced in one country and consumed in another. Because of its location as a trade route, Singapore is able to collect goods from a number of countries in the surrounding region and resell them to merchants and tourists who visit Singapore. This type of trade is referred to as *entrepot trade*. The goods are not manufactured in the country in which they are sold. Entrepot trade is the process of importing goods with the intention of exporting them to other nations. The location of a country or port makes it possible for that particular area to serve as the middleman between the citizens of two or more countries.

Free Trade

As you already know, free trade makes it possible for people throughout the world to live better because each country can specialize in the products in which it has a real or comparative advantage.

The major argument for restricting trade includes national self-sufficiency and protection of "infant" industries.

National Self-sufficiency. The basic argument for national self-sufficiency relates to national defense. A country that is able to produce most of the goods and services needed by its citizens is in a better position at a time of international crisis. A country that is dependent upon the products and services of other nations experiences undue hardships at a time when trade is reduced due to war or to other international emergencies. The problem is to keep the issue of nationalism and national self-sufficiency down to its proper proportion.

Infant Industries. Another argument that is used for restricting foreign trade is to give so-called "infant" industries a chance to develop. A developing nation might, for example, put a tariff (duty or import tax) on manufactured products entering the country from other nations. The argument would be that once the developing nation is able to improve the efficiency of its production, the industry could then compete with similar industries in other nations. The problem here is to be certain that the infant industries involved do, in fact, have the potential to compete with similar industries in other nations. It would be foolish, for example, for countries in the temperate or frigid zones to subsidize the planting of natural rubber under the argument that they could compete favorably with a country like Malaysia, which has a natural advantage in growing rubber. Also, there is a danger involved in continuing the support of the infant industry long after its basic period of adjustment has ended.

Some Additional Arguments Used against Free Trade

In addition to the two main arguments used against free trade, other arguments are sometimes heard.

Trade Leads to Unemployment. The basis of this argument is that if citizens import goods and services from other countries they are not produced domestically. Therefore, workers at home are put out of work as the result of trade.

The argument, of course, must run both directions. Trade makes it possible for a country to increase its productivity and therefore increase its employment rate. Measures to handle unemployment in a country are much more closely tied to fiscal and monetary policies than they are to international trade.

Underdeveloped Nations Have an Advantage in Trade Because of the Low Wages Paid to Workers. This argument says basically that the workers in developed countries will be hurt by competition from workers in lesser developed nations because of lower wage rates in those countries.

A basic answer to this question is that efficiency of production sets wage rates. In the more developed nations, capital goods (tools, machinery, etc.) are used to increase the output of workers. The greater output or efficiency makes it possible for these nations to pay higher wages. As a matter of fact, nations tend to export goods in those industries where wages are highest. The reason for this is quite obvious when you realize that these are the industries in which the country tends to be most efficient.

Tariffs Are a Painless Form of Tax Since They Are Paid by the Citizens of Other Countries. An argument of this sort sounds plausible on the surface. To analyze the question, you must, however, once again refer to the concept of specialization. If a country in a temperate or frigid zone were to place a heavy tariff on Malaysian rubber in order to support such an industry domestically, the consumer of that country would simply have to pay a higher price for natural rubber. Such an example makes it obvious that foreigners (in this case, Malaysians) do not pay the "real" tax on imports. These taxes are, in fact, paid for by the citizens of the country importing the goods. The taxes are paid in the form of higher prices.

Goods Produced at Home Keep the Money at Home. The basis of this argument is that at least when goods and services are produced domestically, the money used in their production stays at home, rather than being shipped abroad. In reality, what happens is that money used to buy goods abroad is usually kept in a bank account held in the name of foreign sellers. The foreign sellers use this account to buy goods. Consequently, exports generate the funds needed for foreigners to import from the country involved.

Balance of Trade

The term *balance of trade* refers to the balance between a nation's exports and its imports. The balance of trade is said to be favorable if the value of exports exceeds the value of imports. An unfavorable balance of trade is said to exist when a nation imports more than it exports. Until 1971, the United States tended to have a favorable balance of trade. In recent years a trade deficit has been common, reaching $14.6 billion, $36.3 billion, and $35.8 billion for 1976, 1977, and 1978 respectively. In September 1978, the United States announced a National Export Policy designed to liberalize trade and to promote U.S. exports.

Balance of Payments

Unless you have the terms clearly in mind, it is easy to confuse *balance of trade* with *balance of payments.* The balance of trade refers strictly to the amount of imports and exports of a nation. The balance of payments, however, includes all financial transactions that take place between a nation and the rest of the world in a given year. The balance of payments includes more than the balance of trade. For example, the balance of payments includes foreign tourist spending, the amount received for shipping services involving other nations, interest and dividends paid on investments by foreigners and to foreigners, expenditures for military activities, loans, grant assistance, and other transfers of funds. Consequently, it is possible for a country to have a favorable balance of trade and an unfavorable balance of payments and vice versa.

The Role of Gold in International Trade

There is no country in the world that operates on a *gold standard*. A gold standard simply means that the money used in a country can be exchanged at any time for a set amount of gold.

In 1933 the United States announced that it would stand ready to buy one ounce of gold for $35. However, U.S. citizens were no longer permitted to exchange their dollars for gold. Gold was to be used only for "backing" the value of the dollar and was actually exchanged only through foreign trade. All other countries set the value of their currencies in the terms of this relationship. All gold transactions were handled by foreign central banks or intergovernmental agencies such as the *World Bank*.

The establishment of an official price for gold, however, did make it possible for governments to always have a recourse if their dollar balances accumulated. For example, if a country were to accumulate more dollars than that needed for imports from the United States, it could ask for the balance in gold.

In 1971, after the United States had suffered a long period of dollar drainages (dollars held in foreign accounts that could be exchanged for gold), the Nixon administration announced that the United States would no longer sell gold to foreign nongovernment holders and reestablished the "official" price of gold at $38 an ounce. In many respects this action basically put to an end the use of gold as a settlement for international accounts. Additionally, this action created two gold markets—or a *two-tiered system* as it was called. There was the official rate of $38 (changed to $42.22 in 1973) an ounce for gold that could be used by official government agencies to settle international trade accounts. But since the nongovernment holders could no longer exchange their gold freely, a "free" or *open market* was established for gold. Since most people felt that the dollar was overvalued, the price of gold on the open market tended to *float* much higher than the "official" rate.

Reducing the importance of gold as a major consideration in settlement of international accounts has been in process for many years. The procedure has been long and tedious. In the late 1960s the *International Monetary Fund (IMF)* established what are called *Special Drawing Rights (SDRs)*. The SDRs are simply paper entities that increase the amount of gold equivalent that nations can use for international trade. In fact, in general financial terms SDRs are often referred to as *paper gold*. The amount of SDRs available to each nation has been adjusted periodically since they were introduced.

The international community has moved slowly but steadily toward *floating exchange rates*. Gold has lost most of its magic in the settlement of international accounts. Most economists and monetary officials believe that Special Drawing Rights will increasingly serve as the basis for a standardized international currency.

Foreign Trade and the Circular Flow

Refer to the circular flow of goods and services as presented in figure 4–6 (p. 47) to assist you in analyzing the effect of foreign trade on an economy.

Note that the circular flow includes all of the components of the GNP: $GNP = C + I + G + F$. As you know, F refers to the exports of a nation minus its imports. It is the net balance of all foreign trade. Note also that exports tend to be an injection into the economy since they bring money into the nation. In a like manner, imports tend to be a leakage since they involve the flow of money to other countries.

At this point, you should review the major flows in an economic system. The leakages include savings, taxation, retained earnings, and imports. The major injections include investment, government spending, and exports. There are three major sections of the economy that affect the general economic level of the nation. These sectors include the private sector (all privately owned businesses), the government sector, and the international sector. In practice these three sectors overlap. A private business will, in fact, be involved in transactions with the government and with international trade. For analysis purposes, however, it is helpful to think of these three groupings as being distinct from one another.

For our analysis, assume a favorable balance of trade. Foreign trade, when F is positive, serves as an injection into the economic system. It is, of course, possible for imports to exceed exports, which would lead to an unfavorable balance of trade. In such a case, the F would be a leakage in the circular flow and have a depressing effect on the economy.

A favorable balance of trade has a multiplier effect on the economy as does any other injection. The increase of funds encourages businesses to employ more productive resources, which, in turn, increase the money payments to the households. Once the households receive these additional payments, they can either (a) save the additional funds or (b) spend these funds for additional goods and services. As you know, the amount of spending and saving is quite predictable. Households tend to save a small portion of their funds but increase their general level of spending. The increase in spending flows to the business firms. Once again business firms adjust by employing additional productive services. The spiral of increased spending continues until either (a) all productive resources are fully employed or (b) savings equal or exceed the amount of additional income flowing to the business firms.

We have now completed an analysis of the components of the economy following the equation $GNP = C + I + G + F$. Our next step is to analyze the role of money and credit in the economy.

nine

Money and Credit

The use and role of money has intrigued people almost from the beginning of time. Money came into being as soon as barter proved to be ineffective. Barter is simply the exchange of goods and services for other goods and services without the use of money. For example, a farmer might exchange two chickens for a certain amount of groceries. Another might exchange ten bushels of wheat for a used plow. Transactions of this type still take place, but it is difficult to become involved in a transaction where the goods exchanged are of equal value. This is particularly true as a society becomes more specialized. For example, a baker with a toothache might have a difficult time locating a dentist who wishes to exchange dental service for a certain amount of bakery goods.

Money was created to help the flow of goods and services. Since money was created by human beings, it is also controlled by human beings, and the role of money has changed drastically over the years.

In this chapter you will find the answers to these questions:

1. What are the major functions of money?
2. What is the function of credit in a society?
3. What are the major kinds of money and credit?
4. What is the role of public debt in an economy?

Functions of Money and Credit

Money in itself has no value. It receives its value in being spent and saved. People do not eat money. They do not wear money. They do not make their homes out of money. Money is used to buy food, clothing, and shelter that a person or family needs. Money is simply an economic institution created to assist in the flow of goods and services.

Functions of Money

The primary functions of money include its serving as (1) a medium of exchange, (2) a store of value, and (3) a standard of value.

Medium of Exchange.   Basically the term *medium of exchange* refers to the fact that people will accept money in return for goods and services. In other words, money is used to help in the exchange of goods and services. Only in the most primitive societies can exchange transactions take place through barter. Once a society becomes specialized, people are dependent upon one another and the need for money exists. As you will learn later in this chapter, many different types of money have been used as a medium of exchange in the past. The key to understanding what is meant by medium of exchange is the word *acceptability*. To serve as a medium of exchange, money must be accepted by the people of the society.

Money is used to help in the exchange of goods and services.

Store of Value.   As you know from previous chapters, people can do two things with money. They can spend it or they can save it. If a person saves money, he or she wants it to have at least as much value in the future as it does at the time that it was put aside. People save money in order to improve their consumption possibilities in the future. Consequently, money put aside today must have value in the future or else people are discouraged from saving. A major problem throughout the world today is that inflation erodes the value of money and discourages saving.

Money set aside (or stored) must have value in the future in order to encourage credit and investment. A person will make a loan (with interest) only if that person feels certain that the amount of money to be returned in the future will have as much value as the amount of money given in the present. Also, as you know from previous discussions, savings can and must be channeled into investments (goods used to make other goods) if an economy is to grow. People will save more money when they feel confident that the value of the money will not decrease over time. Consequently, a key word in understanding the function of money as a store of value is *stability*. Stability refers to the ability of money to retain its value over a period of time. Stability of prices is what gives money its ability to serve as a store of value.

Standard of Value. The term *standard of value* means that money can be used as a common unit of measure when evaluating goods and services. Stated in another way, the standard of value refers to prices. The price of a good or service is an indication of its value to the people in an economy. Prices are a function of what people are willing to pay for goods and services. Without money it would be difficult to have a standard of value. Without money we would have to speak of the value of goods in terms of relationships to other goods. For example, a house might be worth so many automobiles. An automobile, in turn, might be worth so many bushels of corn. A bushel of corn, in turn, might be worth so many haircuts. The whole system would be extremely confusing. It is much simpler to have one standard of value (money) and be able to state the price of goods and services in terms of money.

Functions of Credit

Credit is basically a debt that involves either cash, goods, or services that must be paid back at a future date. Very few individuals or businesses could exist without some form of credit. Without credit it would be necessary for a person to save up the entire amount of money needed to purchase a home before buying one. Also, it would be difficult for a business to expand its operations without the use of credit. Credit serves the economy in many ways.

To Stabilize the Economy. Credit makes it possible for individuals, businesses, and the government to buy goods and services in an even flow though their incomes might be irregular. The government also uses credit to stabilize the economy. During a period of unemployment, for instance, the government will borrow money to build roads, schools, and other public work projects in order to promote economic activity.

To Promote Business Formation. Very few individuals could start a business without the use of credit. The original purchase of land, buildings, and machinery generally requires the use of credit. Sometimes a wholesale firm will grant credit to retailers, or a manufacturer will grant credit to wholesalers thus enabling these businesses to operate with less money.

To Expand Production. Even after a business has been in operation for some time, credit is frequently used to expand production. Businesses receive long-term loans from banks, insurance companies, and other financial institutions. New machinery is purchased, land acquired, and building expansion made through the use of credit. An individual, too, will use credit in order to increase his or her productivity or earning capacity over time. For example, an individual might borrow money to improve his or her education which in time might also improve that person's earning capacity.

To Raise the Level of Living. As mentioned previously, the use of credit makes it possible for a young couple to purchase a home before they have saved the entire amount of money needed. Credit is also used to buy automobiles, furniture, insurance, health services, and other goods and services. Through the use of credit, demand is stimulated which in turn generates production and jobs. Credit makes it possible for people to acquire goods and services and to use them at the same time that they are paying for them.

Kinds of Money and Credit

Over time many different things have been used for money. The Romans used cattle. Many island economies used rice or seashells. Even today some societies use types of money that you might consider unusual. On Yap in Micronesia, for example, some islanders still use large boulders near or in front of their homes to represent their wealth. These rocks or boulders serve as a basis for credit and are generally acceptable as an indication of wealth.

In most economies, however, the money in existence consists of (1) *token coins,* (2) *paper currencies,* and (3) *demand deposits.*

Also, the forms of credit are fairly similar in most economies today.

Types of Money

Probably when you think of money you think of coins or paper currency, but as you will discover in the discussion that follows, the type of money that people carry in their wallets or billfolds actually represents only a small amount of the money used in an economy.

Token Coins. Coins are generally called "token" because they represent only a token of the value they represent. For example, a ten-cent piece does not contain ten cents worth of metal. A fifty-cent piece does not contain fifty cents worth of metal.

Paper Currency. Sometimes called folding money, paper currency is the type of money that a person carries in a billfold or uses for cash purchases. The denominations can range from one dollar to ten thousand dollars. Generally, however, paper currency is in the range of one dollar to one hundred dollars.

Paper currency is issued by the government in response to the needs of individual persons and businesses. The exact process involved will be explained in more detail later. In most developed countries, currency represents only about 20 percent of the total money supply.

Money and Credit 95

Money comes in all shapes, sizes, and textures.

Demand Deposits. The third category of money is demand deposits. You might be more accustomed to thinking of demand deposits by the word *check*. Also, you might be surprised to learn that checks (demand deposits) make up by far the largest component of the total money supply in most countries. Generally, checks represent about 80 percent of the total money supply in countries like the U.S. and Canada. Checks are used because of their convenience and safety. Most people do not carry large sums of currency with them nor do they keep large sums of currency in their homes. Consequently, when large payments are needed, they draw upon funds which have been previously deposited in or borrowed from a bank.

Actually, a check is simply a note or letter to the bank that states: "Take money from my account and pay it to the person whose name is indicated on this note or letter." Every person's signature is different. Therefore, a bank is able to authorize the transfer of funds from one account to another based on the signature of the person making request. Naturally, a bank takes safeguards so that forgeries are avoided.

A check could be written on nearly any type of material, but for the sake of convenience, banks issue checkbooks so that checks can be handled conveniently and efficiently. However, there are cases on record where checks have been written on scraps of paper or, in some cases, rather strange objects indeed. For instance, there is a case on record of a farmer paying a bill by painting a note on the side of a cow and having the cow delivered to the bank. After some delay, the bank honored this check since the signature was authentic. However, anyone using an unorthodox method of check writing must expect the inconvenience of delay, suspicion, and an additional service charge. The point is, however, the check's value is the signature of the authorized person who has money on deposit rather than the form in which the check is presented.

Types of Credit

Credit can be classified in many ways since it is simply a promise to pay back money at a later date. A simple way to classify credit, however, is to divide it into the categories of those people or institutions who use credit. Credit, therefore, consists of (1) government credit, (2) business credit, and (3) consumer credit.

Government Credit. Most governments build highways, schools, hospitals, and other projects through the use of credit. Generally taxes are not adequate to pay for long-term capital expenditures. Taxes are used to keep up the current expenditures such as salaries of government officials, maintenance of property, and the like. However, large projects involve the need for credit. Unexpected emergencies such as national defense also create a demand for credit. The usual procedure for governments to obtain credit is to sell bonds that are paid back at a later date (with interest) out of future taxes. Or a government might borrow money directly from individuals or banks. In some cases, governments receive loans or grants in aid from other governments.

Business Credit. As you know, businesses need credit in order to become established and to expand. Credit is also used in day-to-day operations of a business. For example, a retailer will buy goods from a wholesaler and pay for them thirty, sixty, or ninety days later. A farmer might buy seed from a supplier and pay for it at harvest time.

Businesses also use credit to expand their operations. A business might sell bonds to individuals or institutions that wish to earn interest on their funds or might borrow money directly from banks, insurance companies, or the government.

Consumer Credit. Through the use of credit, individuals are able to use goods and services at the time they are paying for them. For example, few individuals are able to save a sufficient amount of money to pay cash for a home. Also, many individuals engage in "installment buying" whereby they make a down payment on items and pay the remainder in monthly installments that might extend over a year or more of time.

Some individuals use "credit cards." These credit cards authorize an individual to make purchases without paying cash. The customer then pays for the purchases either at the end of the month or through installments. When money is paid in installments there is generally an interest charge added. Businesses might issue credit cards in order to encourage more consumer buying and thereby expand their sales.

A common form of consumer credit is the "open account." Under this type of credit, a consumer buys goods and services from a business for a period of time (usually a month) and pays the balance of the account at the end of that period. Generally, when open accounts are used, business firms do not charge interest. An open account discourages a customer from shopping in other stores and thereby comparing prices. Businesses use open accounts to encourage customers to buy most of their items from them.

Generally, the more risk that is involved in the extension of credit, the higher the rate of interest charged. Credit is based strictly on faith and is available to almost all income categories. However, if the person is a high risk, that person will generally have to pay a larger interest charge. It probably goes without saying that money and credit require careful handling and planning regardless of the size of a person's income. If money and credit are not handled carefully, individuals, businesses, and governments do not achieve their goals.

The Role of Debt

Almost every country has a public debt. The concern for public debt varies from time to time and is often misunderstood by many.

A Comparison of Public and Private Debt

A common economic myth goes something like this: "The federal government is no different from an individual. It cannot continue to spend more money than it takes in without going bankrupt."

There is a tendency for a person to think of public debt the same way he or she thinks of private debt. Actually, the analogy is a poor one. A government's debt differs from private debts in two fundamental respects. First, the government can raise money by taxation, which is obviously not the case for an individual. Second, most government debts are owed to the citizens of the respective country. Stated in another way, citizens of the nation hold government bonds. The holders of these bonds do not normally think of them as "debts." In contrast, when a business or individual owes a debt, it is owed to another business or another individual. Much of the public debt is therefore "internal" and private debt is "external."

By way of analogy, imagine a nation where each individual holds an equal amount of government bonds. Assume also that this particular nation has no external debt; it does not owe any money to any other government or citizens of other countries. Under such a situation, the government taxes the people and, in turn, pays money to the citizens in the form of interest payments. One could almost imagine a situation of the citizens getting together and deciding that they should tear up the bonds since they are taxing themselves to pay themselves interest. This example shows the nature of the internal debt. People do not, of course, hold an equal amount of government bonds. Therefore, public debt transfers money by way of interest from some individuals to others. General tax revenue is used to pay the interest on the bonds and therefore creates a redistribution of income. Also, debt owed to other governments or the citizens of other nations is similar to private debt in that the paying of these funds represents a genuine outflow (leakage from the circular flow) of funds.

The Burden of Debt

Another common economic myth is: "A large public debt puts an unfair burden on future generations." This statement assumes that the debt is transferred from one generation to the next. However, this is not really the case. A person might, for example, inherit a government bond. As you have noted previously, the person who holds a government bond seldom thinks of it as a debt. To that individual, the bond is an asset. However, interest payments on that bond are taken from public tax funds. Consequently, there is a redistribution of income that takes place as a result of public debt. The total amount of the wealth of the nation (assuming no foreign debt) remains, however, the same.

For most nations, the public debt was created as a result of a national emergency such as a war. The real costs of national emergencies are unavoidably paid for at the time in terms of depleted resources, human suffering, and increased efforts by the generation living at that time. The increases in taxation must, of course, continue to future generations to pay the interest to bond holders. However, the bonds that collect interest are also passed on to future generations.

The Size of the Public Debt

You probably also have heard statements such as the following: "The public debt is about $4,000 for every man, woman, and child. This is getting completely out of hand."

A more realistic way of looking at the burden of the debt (in any country) is to compare it with a nation's ability to pay. Stated in another way, this means to compare the debt with the current GNP. This is similar to stating that a person with a large income can afford to carry a larger debt than a person with a small income. The way for a debt to get "completely out of hand" is for it to become so large that the government can no longer afford to pay the interest on the debt.

Debt and Its Effect on Individual Initiative

A statement that reflects a concern for debt's effect on initiative is "The high tax rate caused by the national debt will stifle individual initiative."

Naturally, if the debt becomes so large that the interest rate consumes a good portion of the GNP, a burden is placed upon the citizens in paying the interest charges. Most countries have not reached this level of national debt, and there is really no evidence available to indicate that taxes used to pay the interest on a national debt stifle individual initiative. Surprisingly, an increase in tax might actually stimulate individual initiative under certain conditions. Such a case might include a worker who does some "moonlighting" (taking an extra job) so that he or she is able to meet tax payments. However, if the tax rate becomes so high that a person receives little of the extra income as a result of additional work, it might stifle initiative. The data available are not good enough to enable us to measure the net effect of taxation as it relates to individual initiative. However, for most countries the amount of taxation that is related to the public debt is rather small when compared to other expenditures.

The Role of Debt and Financial Responsibility

A statement that reflects on the role of debt and financial responsibility might go something like this: "Unless the present trend toward unlimited federal debt is reversed, our nation's leaders will resort to more and more irresponsible deficit spending. Internal conflict might even result."

This statement does signal a cause for concern. Government expenditures (like individual expenditures) must be examined carefully and each expenditure must have merit. Government expenditures are not good simply because they are government expenditures. Likewise, government expenditures are not bad simply because they are government expenditures. Governments must plan their expenditures very carefully so that they are of maximum benefit in achieving the goals of the society.

The Use of Debt

A substantial amount of the public debt in most countries is held by the central bank of that country. When a government pays back the debt held by banks, it reduces the bank's reserves and thereby reduces the money supply. The process is generally deflationary. Most banks use government bonds as a form of *near money* that can be transferred to *instant money* on demand. These government bonds are used as reserves in the banking system and held to stabilize the supply of money in a country. If the public debt were wiped out completely, some other form of bank reserves would need to be created to take the place of government bonds.

Chapter 7 is an excellent resource for reviewing the amount of public debt that a nation should carry. A basic objective for most nations is to maintain a high level of employment without inflation. Reduced to its simplest form, this simply means that a government must increase its spending (or issue tax cuts) at the time when unemployment is too high and the economy is sluggish, and decrease its expenditures (or increase taxes) when there is a period of inflation and the economy is overheated. The actual size of the public debt should not be as much of a concern as the status of the economy at the time. The major problem, as you already know, is that it is easier to make a decision to increase spending during the deflationary period than it is to reduce spending during an inflationary period.

A discussion of money and credit leads to an analysis of financial institutions which will be presented in the following chapter.

ten

Financial Institutions

Financial institutions are very important in the day-to-day activities of most individuals and businesses. In this chapter you will learn about financial institutions, their functions, and the services which they provide.

In this chapter you will find the answers to these questions:

1. What are the major forms of financial institutions and what are their functions?
2. What services and loans are offered through financial institutions?
3. How is the Federal Reserve Bank organized?
4. What are the primary purposes of the Federal Reserve Bank?

Common Types of Financial Institutions

Not all financial institutions perform the same functions. The major types of financial institutions include *commercial banks, savings and loan associations, insurance companies,* and *investment corporations.*

Commercial Banks

A commercial bank is owned by its stockholders. The stockholders, in turn, elect a board of directors who manage the affairs of the bank. There is one major difference between a commercial bank and all other types of financial institutions. A commercial bank is the only financial institution that is authorized to have checking accounts. Therefore, if a financial institution offers the services of a checking account, it is a commercial bank. Most commercial banks also make short-term loans to individuals, generally ranging from thirty to ninety days. Most commercial banks also make long-term loans to businesses that will extend over a period of fifteen or twenty years or more. In addition, most commercial banks are also authorized to maintain savings accounts on which they pay interest to the depositors on the savings. These savings are then used to extend the loan capacity of the bank.

Savings and Loan Associations

A savings and loan association is not a bank. It does not, therefore, make available the services of a checking account. This type of financial institution is concerned primarily with long-term savings and long-term loans. The money it uses for loans is in the form of *share capital.* Placing money in a savings and loan association is essentially the same as buying a share of stock in a corporation. The loans made by a savings and loan association are usually in the form of mortgages for homes and industrial purposes. Reserve funds are generally invested in government securities.

Insurance Companies

The basic purpose of an insurance company is to provide protection against risk. The money paid into insurance companies (called *premiums*) is available for a long-term mortgage loan or loans to businesses or to purchase government securities. Insurance companies frequently have large sums of money available since premiums are paid in over a relatively long period of time and accumulated by the insurance company. For example, a person who buys a life insurance policy seldom dies immediately following that purchase; therefore, insurance companies tend to specialize in large long-term loans.

Investment Corporations

Investment corporations deal primarily in the purchase and sale of corporate securities. The investment corporation will purchase the securities of a corporation for a given price and sell them in turn to the public for a higher price. In this way a corporation seeking to sell large amounts of securities to the general public deals with only one financial institution.

Credit Unions

A credit union is a cooperative that accepts money from its depositors and makes loans to its members. Credit unions are usually organized for the individuals within a particular business firm, geographical location, or other identifying characteristic. Credit unions will often make loans that are somewhat riskier than those made by other financial institutions since all transactions are limited to its members. Also, since a credit union is a cooperative, it is a nonprofit institution and when operated efficiently can make loans at a lower rate of interest than possible through other financial institutions.

Consumer Finance Companies

The primary purpose of a consumer finance company is to lend relatively small amounts of money to wage earners and others of moderate means who do not have an established credit rating. Loans made by consumer finance companies tend to be riskier than those of other financial institutions. Consequently, the interest rates charged tend to be higher than those of a commercial bank, a savings and loan association, an insurance company, a credit union, or most other financial institutions. Consumer finance companies accept deposits and pay interest. The interest rates paid on deposits are frequently higher than those paid by other financial institutions.

Other Financial Institutions

Various other financial organizations are possible. Any type of institution that accepts deposits, pays interest, or makes loans can be considered a financial institution.

Services Offered Through a Commercial Bank

You are already familiar with a number of services offered through commercial banks. In this section of the chapter, you will examine some of these services in more detail.

Checking Accounts

Commercial banks accept *deposits* from businesses and individuals who can, in turn, demand those funds on request. This service is called a *checking account service,* and the deposits are called *demand deposits.* A demand to withdraw funds is done in the form of a check, which is simply an order by the depositor to pay the funds to the person or institution named as the *payee* on the check.

Most business transactions are done by check. Money placed in a checking account is safe from loss or theft. Therefore, many people prefer to have their money deposited in a bank and to use checks to pay bills rather than to use cash. Checks are convenient, safe, and easily handled.

Stopping Payment of a Check

If a check is lost or stolen, the bank should be notified immediately so that payment of the check can be stopped. Usually, there is some urgency in notifying the bank; consequently, most banks will accept an oral (e.g., a telephone call) order to *stop payment* of a check if the oral order is followed immediately by a written order on a special form provided by the bank.

Bank Draft

A *bank draft* is a check drawn by a bank on funds that it has on deposit in another bank. This form of check is sometimes used when an individual is not known by the payee. Most people and businesses will accept a check of a bank more readily than they will a personal check from an individual.

Certified Checks

A *certified check* is an ordinary check with one major difference. The drawer of the check presents the check to the bank before it is presented to the payee. The bank, in turn, deducts the amount of the check from the depositor's account and stamps or writes on the check (certifies) that the check is valid. The certification by the bank makes the check an obligation of the bank rather than of the depositor. Stated in another way, the bank guarantees the payment of the certified check.

Certified checks are used for the same reason that bank drafts are used. The bank charges a small service fee for certifying checks.

Cashier's Check

A *cashier's check* is a check that a bank draws against its own account. A cashier's check is used by a bank to pay the bills of the bank. A cashier's check can be purchased by an individual and be used in the same fashion as a certified check or bank draft.

Traveler's Check

People who travel usually do not like to carry along large sums of cash. Also, they frequently find it difficult to cash personal checks since they are not known by the firms and individuals with whom they do business while traveling. Consequently, some banks (and other financial organizations) issue a special type of check called the *traveler's check*. A traveler's check is guaranteed valid by the agency issuing it. Consequently, traveler's checks are more readily accepted than personal checks. Usually, the buyer of traveler's checks pays a small fee for the service. When a traveler's check is purchased, the customer signs his or her name on the check. At the time the check is presented in payment of a bill, the person must match his or her original signature with an additional signature on the check. Also, most traveler's checks are guaranteed by the issuing agency and, if lost, the person who has purchased the checks can receive a total refund of the amount of money represented by the checks.

Other Bank Services

As you already know, most banks maintain *savings accounts*. These accounts are convenient and safe for a person who wishes to deposit money and earn interest with minimum risk. Because the risk is so small, interest rates on savings accounts tend also to be less than interest rates on many other types of investments.

Some banks also issue time deposits, or as they are generally called, *certificates of deposit (CDs)*. Certificates of deposit generally earn a higher rate of interest than a regular savings account since the depositor must agree to keep the money in the bank for a specified period of time—such as three months, six months, a year, or more. Usually, certificates of deposit are sold in multiples of one thousand dollars.

Another service offered by many banks is that of providing *safety deposit boxes* in the bank that are available to customers on a rental basis. Such a box provides safety against theft, loss, or fire. Many people (and businesses) use safety deposit boxes for storing valuables such as jewelry or important legal documents.

Some banks also provide financial and tax advice for their customers. In some instances, banks even maintain tax specialists who will prepare (for a fee) income tax returns for their customers.

They also help travelers by exchanging local currency for foreign currency when such a service is needed. In addition, some banks will arrange for deposits by their customers in banks in other countries.

More and more banks (particularly in developed nations) operate a charge account service. The bank issues a credit card that can be used in all stores and businesses which participate in the plan initiated by the bank. The customer with a bank credit card receives one bill from the bank at the end of the month. Ordinarily, the bank will also make it possible for the customer to pay the balance due in installment payments. Naturally, when the customer pays through the installment plan, the bank charges an interest rate for this service.

Some banks also provide customers with the type of service that is called *line of credit*. A line of credit essentially means that a customer is automatically authorized to write checks to a certain amount that exceeds the amount in the customer's account. Essentially what this means is that the bank stands ready upon written orders (a check by the customer) to provide an instant loan to that customer. This also is referred to as an overdraft facility.

Most commercial banks also sell government bonds. Some banks also serve as the brokers for the purchase and sale of securities issued by business firms.

Obtaining Personal Loans

Many people occasionally find it necessary to borrow money for a period of time ranging from a few days to many years. The longer the period of the loan, the more important the interest charges involved become.

Short-term loans are made for such emergencies as unexpected medical expenses, hospital bills, the purchase or repair of household equipment, educational expenses, holidays, and the like. Longer term loans are often made for the purchase of a home, a permanent addition, improvements to a home, or for establishing a business.

Where Should You Borrow Money?

Before borrowing money you should shop for your loan the same way that you would shop for the purchase of other goods and services. The advantages and disadvantages of dealing with a particular financial institution depend upon the

Financial Institutions

RESIDENTIAL LOAN APPLICATION

MORTGAGE APPLIED FOR	☐ Conventional ☐ VA	☐ FHA	Amount $	Interest Rate %	No. of Months	Monthly Payment Principal & Interest $	Escrow/Impounds (to be collected monthly) ☐ Taxes ☐ Hazard Ins. ☐ Mtg. Ins.

Prepayment Option

SUBJECT PROPERTY

Property Street Address	City	County	State	Zip	No. Units

Legal Description (Attach description if necessary) — Year Built

Purpose of Loan: ☐ Purchase ☐ Construction-Permanent ☐ Construction ☐ Refinance ☐ Other (Explain)

Complete this line if Construction-Permanent or Construction Loan	Lot Value Data Year Acquired $	Original Cost $	Present Value (a) $	Cost of Imps. (b) $	Total (a + b) $	ENTER TOTAL AS PURCHASE PRICE IN DETAILS OF ☐ PURCHASE.

Complete this line if a Refinance Loan Year Acquired / Original Cost / Amt. Existing Liens $ / $ / $	Purpose of Refinance	Describe Improvements [ ] made [ ] to be made Cost: $

Title Will Be Held In What Name(s) — Manner In Which Title Will Be Held

Source of Down Payment and Settlement Charges

This application is designed to be completed by the borrower(s) with the lender's assistance. The Co-Borrower Section and all other Co-Borrower questions must be completed and the appropriate box(es) checked if ☐ another person will be jointly obligated with the Borrower on the loan, or ☐ the Borrower is relying on income from alimony, child support or separate maintenance or on the income or assets of another person as a basis for repayment of the loan, or ☐ the Borrower is married and resides, or the property is located, in a community property state.

BORROWER				CO-BORROWER			
Name		Age	School Yrs	Name		Age	School Yrs
Present Address No. Years ☐ Own ☐ Rent				Present Address No. Years ☐ Own ☐ Rent			
Street				Street			
City/State/Zip				City/State/Zip			
Former address if less than 2 years at present address				Former address if less than 2 years at present address			
Street				Street			
City/State/Zip				City/State/Zip			
Years at former address ☐ Own ☐ Rent				Years at former address ☐ Own ☐ Rent			
Marital ☐ Married ☐ Separated Status ☐ Unmarried (incl. single, divorced, widowed)		DEPENDENTS OTHER THAN LISTED BY CO-BORROWER NO AGES		Marital ☐ Married ☐ Separated Status ☐ Unmarried (incl. single, divorced, widowed)		DEPENDENTS OTHER THAN LISTED BY BORROWER NO AGES	
Name and Address of Employer		Years employed in this line of work or profession? ____ years Years on this job ____ ☐ Self Employed*		Name and Address of Employer		Years employed in this line of work or profession? ____ years Years on this job ____ ☐ Self Employed*	
Position/Title	Type of Business			Position/Title	Type of Business		
Social Security Number***	Home Phone	Business Phone		Social Security Number***	Home Phone	Business Phone	

GROSS MONTHLY INCOME				MONTHLY HOUSING EXPENSE**			DETAILS OF PURCHASE	
Item	Borrower	Co-Borrower	Total	Rent	PRESENT	PROPOSED	Do Not Complete If Refinance	
Base Empl. Income	$	$	$	First Mortgage (P&I)		$	a. Purchase Price	$
Overtime				Other Financing (P&I)			b. Total Closing Costs (Est.)	
Bonuses				Hazard Insurance			c. Prepaid Escrows (Est.)	
Commissions				Real Estate Taxes			d. Total (a + b + c)	$
Dividends/Interest				Mortgage Insurance			e. Amount This Mortgage	( )
Net Rental Income				Homeowner Assn. Dues			f. Other Financing	( )
Other† (Before completing, see notice under Describe Other Income below.)				Other			g. Other Equity	( )
				Total Monthly Pmt	$	$	h. Amount of Cash Deposit	( )
				Utilities			i. Closing Costs Paid by Seller	( )
Total	$	$	$	Total	$	$	j. Cash Reqd. For Closing (Est.)	$

DESCRIBE OTHER INCOME

☐ B—Borrower C—Co-Borrower

NOTICE: † Alimony, child support, or separate maintenance income need not be revealed if the Borrower or Co-Borrower does not choose to have it considered as a basis for repaying this loan.

	Monthly Amount
	$

IF EMPLOYED IN CURRENT POSITION FOR LESS THAN TWO YEARS COMPLETE THE FOLLOWING

B/C	Previous Employer/School	City/State	Type of Business	Position/Title	Dates From/To	Monthly Income
						$

THESE QUESTIONS APPLY TO BOTH BORROWER AND CO-BORROWER

If a "yes" answer is given to a question in this column, explain on an attached sheet.	Borrower Yes or No	Co-Borrower Yes or No	If applicable, explain Other Financing or Other Equity (provide addendum if more space is needed).
Have you any outstanding judgments? In the last 7 years, have you been declared bankrupt?			
Have you had property foreclosed upon or given title or deed in lieu thereof?			
Are you a co-maker or endorser on a note?			

Personal loans may be obtained from savings and loan firms.

precise conditions involved at the time. When you are shopping for a loan, you must consider the reliability of the lender, the "real" cost of the loan (including service charges, special fees, etc.), and the general terms of consideration that are involved.

Types of Loans

There are basically two ways to repay a loan. You can repay the entire amount of the loan in a lump sum along with the interest due, or you can repay the loan in regular installments.

There are also different types of security arrangements for loans. One type is an unsecured loan that is based upon your signature only. In this case, the lender relies on your character and goodwill to repay the loan. Naturally, if you do not make the payment, the lender has legal recourse against you. Another type of loan is a secured loan. When a loan is secured, the lender has a legal right to take possession of a certain kind of property called *collateral* (for example, an automobile, business securites, or furniture) in the event that you are unable to pay the loan. In this way, the lender has a claim against the property until your loan is repaid.

Sometimes a lender also requests the signature of an additional person who agrees to take on the responsibility to pay the loan in the event that the person who was granted the loan is unable to do so. This person is called the *co-signer* or *co-maker* of the loan. A father might, for example, co-sign a loan for one of his children.

Interest Rates

Interest rates vary according to the types of loan and the risk involved.

Borrowing from Banks. Generally, when a person's credit rating is good, he or she is able to receive a loan from a commercial bank at a minimum interest rate. Interest rates fluctuate widely from time to time and from country to country. In general, however, interest rates charged by commercial banks tend to be lower than interest rates charged by most other financial institutions. This is true because commercial banks seldom enter into a loan arrangement that is of high risk.

Borrowing from Savings and Loan Associations. Savings and loan associations are designed primarily to make loans for the purchase of homes. This type of financial institution tends to promote savings and to encourage home ownership. The savings of the depositors are used to make loans to people interested in buying homes. A savings and loan association will charge borrowers a slightly higher percentage of interest than it pays depositors. Consequently, if depositors are paid 7 or 8 percent interest, the interest charged to borrowers will tend to be 10 or 11 percent (or more) on home loans.

Borrowing from Life Insurance Companies. All life insurance policies (with the exception of term insurance) accumulate a cash value as premiums are paid year after year. A term policy simply protects a person against the possibility of loss of life and has no savings element in it. Consequently, it does not accumulate a cash value.

Once a life insurance policy accumulates a cash value, the holder of the policy is generally able to borrow money against the policy. A person who borrows money against his or her life insurance policy must realize, however, that the insurance protection is reduced by the amount of the loan. Loans by insurance companies tend to have a lower interest rate because a person is essentially borrowing his or her own money.

Borrowing from Consumer Finance Companies. Consumer finance companies serve an important role in making it possible for a person to receive a loan when he or she might otherwise find it difficult to obtain money for unexpected emergencies or other legitimate purposes. The amount of loans made available through consumer finance companies tends to be small, and the period of time for repayment is typically less than two years. The risk of loans made by consumer finance companies tends to be greater. It is not unusual for a consumer finance company to charge rates that are much higher than the rates charged by a commercial bank.

Borrowing from Credit Unions. In order to borrow money from a credit union, a person must be a member. Membership in a credit union is obtained by buying one or more shares, usually issued at a nominal fee. Loans are simply made out of the funds deposited by the members. Practices of a credit union vary so widely that it is difficult to make generalizations. Some credit unions are large and financially secure enough to make rather substantial loans. Credit unions tend to make loans for the purchase of such items as furniture, for household repairs and renovations, or for automobiles. Usually the loans are made for a period of less than five years.

Other Types of Borrowing. In addition to the types of borrowing discussed above, a person might also borrow from family, friends, pawnbrokers, or unauthorized moneylenders (called *loan sharks*). All types of borrowing must be carefully thought through and handled with care.

The Federal Reserve Bank

Money and credit do not manage themselves. Consequently, most countries have established a central bank. The central bank of the United States is the *Federal Reserve Bank,* which was established in 1913 and modified during the depression of the 1930s. The aim of the Federal Reserve Bank is to (1) provide for and control the flow of money and credit, (2) facilitate economic growth, (3) assist in stabilizing prices, and (4) help the nation maintain an orderly flow in international payments. The actual functions of the Federal Reserve in regulating the flow of money and credit will be discussed in the following chapter. This chapter is concerned primarily with the organizational mechanism of the Federal Reserve.

The governing powers of the Federal Reserve system rest with the *Board of Governors.* This board consists of seven people appointed by the President of the United States and confirmed by the Senate. Each member of the Board of Governors serves a fourteen-year term, and these terms are staggered to assure continuity of policy. The Board of Governors is assisted by two major committees:

108 Financial Institutions

1. The *Federal Open Market Committee* regulates the buying and selling of government securities in the open market. This committee consists of the seven governors plus five presidents of district Federal Reserve banks. The committee meets in New York, and each member serves a three-year term.
2. The *Federal Advisory Council* advises on general banking policy. This council consists of twelve bankers selected from the twelve Federal Reserve districts. The primary function of the council is advisory and each member serves for a one year term.

The district Federal Reserve banks are often referred to as the *banker's bank*. Commercial bankers use the district Federal Reserve banks in much the same manner that depositors use a commercial bank. The Federal Reserve district banks are owned by commercial banks in their respective district but operate in the public interest. Thus, even though the commercial banks own the Federal Reserve district banks, they do not exercise control over them. The Federal Reserve district banks operate as independent institutions and as *quasi-governmental* units. Their operations are not conducted for profit and any excess of receipts over expenditures are deposited with the U.S. Treasury. Each Federal Reserve district bank has a nine-member board of directors consisting of bankers, businesspeople, farmers, and others. To avoid banker domination of policy, not all directors are bankers.

The structure of the Federal Reserve system is shown in figure 10–1.

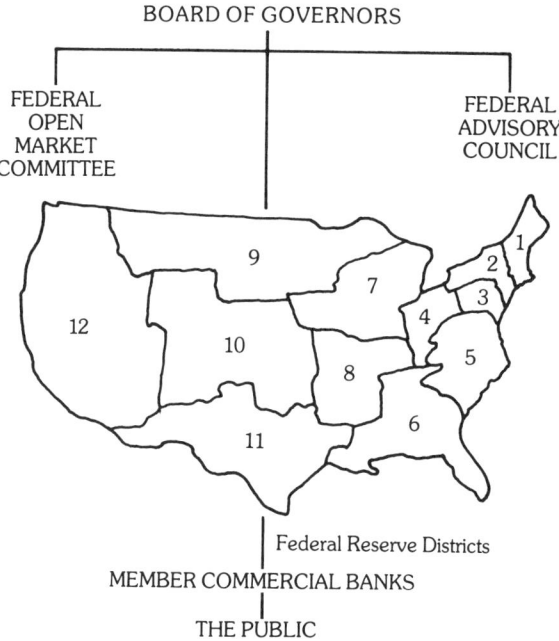

Figure 10–1. *Structure of the Federal Reserve.*

National versus State Banks

In the United States a bank can be chartered either by the federal government or by a state government. There are approximately 14,000 commercial banks in the United States. Of these, nearly 4,700 are *national banks*. A national bank must be a member of the Federal Reserve system. *State banks* can, however, opt not to join the Federal Reserve system if they so wish. Approximately 2,000 of the 9,300 state banks are members of the Federal Reserve system. Therefore, only about half of all commercial banks in the United States are members of the Federal Reserve system, but they tend to be the larger commercial banks, conducting approximately 85 percent of all banking business done in the country.

Privileges and Responsibilities of Federal Reserve Members

A bank that is a member of the Federal Reserve system has the right to (1) borrow money from Federal Reserve bank, (2) use Federal Reserve banks for collecting checks and transferring funds, (3) obtain currency for day-to-day operations, (4) use the informational facilities provided by a Federal Reserve bank, (5) participate in the election of the board of directors, and (6) receive dividends on the stock that the bank has on deposit in a Federal Reserve bank.

Each commercial bank that is a member of the Federal Reserve system must deposit with the Federal Reserve 3 percent of its capital stock. Another 3 percent is on call by the Federal Reserve at any time that it might be needed.

A bank that is a member of the Federal Reserve system must (1) maintain required reserves with the Federal Reserve either as deposits or as cash in its vault, (2) comply with various banking regulations determined by the Federal Reserve, and (3) be subject to examination by the controller of the currency.

Now that we have completed a discussion of money, credit, and financial institutions, we will conclude our analysis with a discussion of monetary policy which follows in chapter 11.

eleven

Money and Monetary Policy

As you know, the federal government is a money-creating institution. The federal government mints coins and prints the paper money that is in circulation. However, as you also know, demand deposits constitute most of the money supply. Demand deposits are not created by the government. In this chapter, we shall examine how demand deposits come into being and the effect that the quantity of money in circulation has on general economic activity. Further, we shall examine how the supply of money and credit may be regulated.

In this chapter you will find the answers to these questions:

1. How do commercial banks create money?
2. What is meant by the money multiplier?
3. How do central banks control money and credit by making changes in the reserve requirements of member banks?
4. How do the central banks control money and credit by changing the discount rate?
5. What are open market operations?
6. How does a change in a margin requirement to buy securities affect money and credit?
7. How do central banks restrict or encourage consumer credit?
8. What is meant by "moral suasion?"

How Commercial Banks Create Money

You are already familiar with the basic role of commercial banks in an economy. In this chapter, you will learn more about the significant role that commercial banks play in creating money. Before examining the process in detail, however, it is well to review certain definitions and to set assumptions.

Definitions

The term *liabilities* refers to the money that a person or an individual owes. In our case, demand deposits are liabilities of the bank since the bank owes its depositors that amount.

The term *assets* refers to the amount of money or goods that an institution or an individual owns. In our example, the assets of a bank are the reserves that it has on deposit with the Federal Reserve Bank (Fed) and its loans. The Fed owes the bank the amount of the reserves on deposit, and customers of the bank owe the bank the amount of loans that the bank has made to them.

The *reserve requirement* is the percentage of its total deposits that a bank is required to maintain in reserve at the Fed. This means that banks must have on deposit with the Fed a certain percentage (for example, 20 percent) of all of their demand deposits.

The term *total reserves* refers to the amount of deposits that a bank has with the Fed. For example, the total reserves of a bank would be the amount of money that the bank has on deposit with the Fed.

The term *required reserves* refers to the actual dollar amount that a bank needs to meet its reserve requirement with the Fed.

The term *excess reserves* refers to the actual dollar amount of deposits at the Fed that is above the dollar amount necessary to meet the required reserve ratio.

The Setting

For the sake of simplicity, we shall simply refer to the commercial banks by a letter designation. The banks will, therefore, be Bank A, Bank B, and Bank C, and so on. All the banks are members of the Federal Reserve System. For the purpose of our illustration we will assume that the reserve requirement (ratio) for all banks is 10 percent and that there are no excess reserves in the banking system. Or stated in another way, all the banks are "loaned up."

Transactions

Assume that Bank A receives a $100 deposit in currency from one of its customers. The deposits in Bank A have, therefore, increased by $100. Bank A must, in order to meet the legal reserve requirement of the Fed, forward a minimum of $10 to the Fed. However, Bank A wishes to improve its loaning capacity and sends the entire $100 to the Fed. Consequently, Bank A now has $90 in excess reserves available to lend. Bank A's position can be illustrated as shown in chart 11–1.

Chart 11–1. *The Creation of Money*

Bank	Liabilities		Assets	
	Deposits	Total Reserves	Required Reserves	Excess Reserves
A	100	100	10	90

Assume that Bank A makes a loan of $90 to a customer who uses the money to pay a debt. The person receiving the $90 deposits this amount in Bank B. Bank B's total deposits have now increased by $90. It must, therefore, send $9 to the Fed to meet the required reserve ratio of 10 percent. Bank B, however, wishes to improve its loaning capacity and forwards the entire $90. Bank B now has $81 dollars in excess reserves and can, of course, make loans for that amount. Bank A, however, in making a loan of $90 has depleted its excess reserves with the Fed. Stated in another way, the total reserves that Bank A has on deposit with the Fed is exactly equal to its required reserves. Consequently, Bank A is no longer in the position to make any additional loans.

Assume that Bank B makes the loan of $81 which, in turn, is eventually deposited in Bank C. Bank C must forward 10 percent of its new deposit to the Fed to meet its legal reserve requirement of 10 percent. (The actual amount would, of course, be $8.10. For simplicity you can round off all numbers to the nearest dollar.) Assume, however, that Bank C forwards the entire $81, thereby creating $73 in excess reserves that can be loaned out. Bank B, however, in making a loan of $81 has depleted its excess reserves with the Fed.

You have probably already sensed how the process can be continued to greater length. Each bank must use a portion (10 percent) of the original $100 as required reserves against the money deposited with it. Bank A needs $10 in required reserves, Bank B needs $9, Bank C needs $8, and if the process were continued to Bank D, the required reserves would be $7. Notice that at each step the amount of the required reserves becomes less. This is true since it is always reduced by 10 percent.

Assume that the transactions continue through a number of banks. This situation can be illustrated as shown in chart 11–2.

Chart 11–2. *The Creation of Money*

Bank	Liabilities		Assets	
	Deposits	Total Reserves	Required Reserves	Excess Reserves
A	100	10	10	0
B	90	9	9	0
C	81	8	8	0
D	73	7	7	0
E	66	7	7	0
F	59	6	6	0
Total at Infinity	1000	100	100	0

Note that with each round of transactions there is an increase in the money supply. In the illustration given above, we have terminated the round of transactions with Bank F. Obviously, you could continue these transactions to infinity. At the latest stages, however, the amount of new money created would be extremely small. Actually, there is an easy way to determine how much could be created by a deposit of $100 when the reserve ratio is 10 percent and the transactions were, in fact, carried to infinity. You are already familiar with the "multiplier" and the same line of reasoning applies to the "bank multiplier." Consequently, with a reserve requirement of 10 percent, a deposit of $100 has the potential of creating $1,000 since the multiplier is 10. In a like manner, a 20 percent reserve requirement would produce a multiplier of 5. If you have any confusion regarding the determination of the multiplier or the process involved, you should review chapter 4.

Monetary Policy

Monetary policy refers to regulating the cost and availability of money and credit to promote economic growth and price stability and to reduce unemployment. The agency charged with initiating and enforcing monetary policy in most countries is a central bank which operates as a quasi-governmental agency.

Major Monetary Controls

The Federal Reserve System influences the volume of credit and money by (1) making changes in the reserve requirements of member banks, (2) making changes in the discount rate available to member banks, and (3) by engaging in open market operations.

Changes in the Reserve Requirement. In the United States, affiliated Federal Reserve banks conduct about 85 percent of all the banking done in the country. The Fed requires that a certain percentage of demand deposits of each affiliated commercial bank be placed on deposit with it. The Fed, in turn, reserves the right to change the percentage amount of deposit required. A member bank then can make loans only in the amount of the *excess* reserves it has in the Federal Reserve Bank. Loans cannot be made from the *required* reserves. In this way, the Fed controls the amount of credit available to customers of commercial banks.

Assume for example that Mr. Jones deposits $1,000 into the account he has at Bank A. If the Fed has set a reserve requirement of 10 percent, Bank A must deposit a minimum of $100 with the Fed if we assume that Bank A has no excess reserves on deposit with the Fed at the time.

Assume, however, that Bank A wishes to accumulate some excess reserves to improve its loaning capacity. Bank A, therefore, deposits with the Fed $200. The account of Bank A with the Fed is then as follows:

Total Reserves	Required Reserves	Excess Reserves
$200	$100	$100

At this point, Bank A has excess reserves of $100 and is able to make loans of that amount. A loan of $100 can set off a "multiplier effect" that could expand loans throughout the banking system of $100. You are already familiar with the principle of the multiplier and in the previous section you saw precisely how a deposit of $100 can multiply into $1,000 when the reserve requirement is 10 percent.

Now assume there is an inflationary tendency and the Board of Governors of the Federal Reserve is concerned that prices are rising too rapidly. Before Bank A has an opportunity to loan out the $100 that it has on deposit with the Fed as excess reserves, the Fed changes the required reserve ratio to 20 percent. This action wipes out the entire amount of Bank A's excess reserves (the new required reserve being $200) and it can no longer loan out the $100.

After a change in the reserve ratio from 10 percent to 20 percent, Bank A's account with the Fed is as follows:

Total Reserves	Required Reserves	Excess Reserves
$200	$200	—0—

Thus, by raising or lowering the reserve requirement a central bank can absorb or set free reserves, thereby affecting a member bank's ability to make loans. Remember also that loans are deposited in the account of commercial banks and become demand deposits. Demand deposits, as you know, are a form of money. In fact, they are the major source of the money supply of most countries. Consequently, by raising or lowering the reserve requirement, a central bank is able to expand or contract the money supply.

Change in a Discount Rate. District Federal Reserve banks are sometimes referred to as banker's banks. A commercial bank uses the service of its district Federal Reserve bank in a manner similar to the way individuals and business firms use the service of a commercial bank. Just as individuals and business firms go to commercial banks for loans, commercial banks go to the Fed for a loan when they need to improve their reserve status or when they need to meet unexpected deposit withdrawals. Naturally a commercial bank (like an individual or business firm) must pay interest on the money it receives as a loan. The interest charged by the Fed to a commercial bank is called the *discount rate.*

In the example given above, it would appear that Bank A would not be able to make any loans since it has no excess reserves. Assume, however, that Bank A, in order to make a loan, borrows $100 from the Fed. After borrowing $100, the position of Bank A with the Fed is as follows:

Total Reserves	Required Reserves	Excess Reserves
$300	$200	$100

Naturally, Bank A will have to repay the loan to the Fed at a future date with interest. The Fed can encourage or discourage loans from its account by changing the interest rate—called the discount rate—that it charges commercial banks. When the discount rate is low, commercial banks are more likely to borrow money from the Fed. A higher discount rate discourages commercial banks from borrowing from the Fed. Therefore, a low discount rate tends to have the effect of encouraging commercial banks to accumulate excess reserves. A high discount rate discourages the accumulation of excess reserves by commercial banks. The amount of excess reserves, as you already know, establishes a commercial bank's ability to make loans to its customers.

If a commercial bank must pay a high discount rate when it receives a loan from the Fed, it, in turn, will tend to charge a higher interest rate to its customers. When the interest rate at a commercial bank is high, it tends to discourage individuals and businesses from borrowing from the commercial bank. When the interest rate at a commercial bank is low, it tends to encourage individuals and businesses to borrow. Thus, the Federal Reserve System is able to encourage or discourage the amount of loans made in a country by raising or lowering the discount rate.

Open Market Operations. The third major tool of monetary policy consists of the buying or selling of government securities that are held by the Federal Reserve. This tool is used extensively in the United States. Essentially it involves the buying and selling of government debts. Commercial banks use government securities as a form of "near money." Federal Reserve banks accept government securities as deposits to fulfill the required reserves of commercial banks. The federal government also sells securities directly to the Federal Reserve. Or stated in another way, the government receives funds from the Federal Reserve. The Federal Reserve is, therefore, in a position to buy and sell government securities. These buying and selling transactions directly affect the loaning capacity of member banks.

A simple illustration will show how the process works. The Fed might buy a government bond from a commercial bank, a household, or a business firm. For purposes of illustration, assume that the central bank purchased a $100 government bond from Ms. Smith. In return for the bond, Ms. Smith receives a check of $100. She immediately deposits the $100 in Bank A. Bank A, therefore, credits Ms. Smith's account with an additional $100. Assume that Bank A forwards the check to the Fed in an attempt to improve its loaning capacity by increasing its excess reserves.

If you assume that no other transactions have taken place since our last illustration involving the account of Bank A with the Fed, the reserve position of Bank A is now as follows:

Total Reserves	Required Reserves	Excess Reserves
$400	$220	$180

Consequently, the purchase of a government bond by the Fed increased Bank A's lending ability by $80. Remember also that the $80 has the capacity to multiply as it moves through the banking system. Therefore, the purchase of government securities by the Fed tends to increase the amount of credit available in a country. From your past readings you know that such a policy would be used during a deflationary period when the Fed wishes to encourage additional spending. The process of buying government securities by the Fed is used to create more business activity, stimulate economic growth, and to reduce unemployment. An excellent review of this process is to trace this activity through the circular flow diagram presented in chapter 4.

Assume, however, that the Fed is concerned about inflation and wishes to discourage credit in the economy. Such a policy would be used when the economy is overheated and prices are rising more rapidly than production.

For illustrative purposes assume that the Fed sells a $100 government bond to Mr. Barnes. In order to purchase this bond Mr. Barnes writes a check on Bank A and forwards this check to the Fed. Once again if you assume that no other transactions took place since the last illustration, Bank A's reserve position with the Fed is as follows:

Total Reserves	Required Reserves	Excess Reserves
$300	$200	$100

In this illustration, the excess reserves of Bank A are reduced by $80 which, in turn, lowers its lending power. Consequently, when the Fed wishes to discourage credit to counteract inflation, it sells government securities.

The process of buying and selling government securities is called "open market operations" because the Fed makes government securities available to any potential customer. They are, in fact, bought and sold in the open market.

Minor Monetary Controls

The major monetary controls discussed thus far are sometimes referred to as quantitative tools of monetary policy. The central banks of most countries also employ certain types of minor or "qualitative tools" to control the cost and availability of credit. The principal types of monetary controls under this category include (1) changes in the margin requirements, (2) control of consumer credit, and (3) moral suasion.

Margin Requirements. As you know from chapter 6, business firms issue securities generally referred to as stocks and bonds. Also, as you know, the securities of major business firms are bought and sold through institutions called stock exchanges.

In order to specualte in the stock market, individuals and business firms will often borrow money to purchase the securities. For example, if Ms. Green wishes to purchase a business security that is selling for $100 and she has only $10, she might borrow the $90 so that she can complete the transaction. Her hope is, of course, that the security will increase in price and that she can sell it at a higher price and repay the loan of $90. If, however, the market crashes (has a sudden drop in price), she is in no position to pay back the $90 loan through the sale of the security. In such a case, she will be forced to sell other assets in order to repay the loan. If many people must sell off personal assets in order to repay the loans, prices are deflated and a general recession (down turn in prices) or even a depression (drastic decrease in prices coupled with a high rate of unemployment) is created.

In 1929 there was a major stock market crash that developed in the United States. The repercussions of this crash were felt throughout the world. In fact, a state of depression existed in much of the world for many years following the stock market crash. One of the basic reasons for the stock market crash in 1929 was the excessive use of credit (borrowing) in the purchasing of securities.

To avoid stock market crashes and excessive speculation in the market, most of the central banks of most countries established a margin requirement for the purchase of securities. A margin requirement is simply the percentage of the total cost of the security that a buyer must provide from his or her own funds to purchase the security. A margin requirement of 90 percent, for instance, means that the purchaser of the security must put up $90 in cash for every $100 of securities purchased. Obviously, the security buyer is then allowed to borrow only $10.

The central banks of most nations change the margin requirement for the purchase of securities based upon the economic conditions that exist at the time. If the monetary authorities of the central bank wish to encourage the purchase of business securities, they lower the margin requirement. For example, a margin requirement of 50 percent encourages the purchase of more securities than a margin of 100 percent. Central banks frequently change the margin requirement of securities within the range of 50 percent to 100 percent.

Control of Consumer Credit. The central banks of many countries are authorized to impose restrictions on the use of consumer credit. A central bank might, for example, have the authority to establish the minimum down payment that a consumer must make on a home, an automobile, or household appliances. Central banks might also have the authority to set the length of time within which installment loans must be repaid. Obviously, when consumers are required to make larger down payments, their buying potential is restricted. In a similar manner, if they must pay back the loan in a shorter period of time, their credit purchases are discouraged.

Central banks will tend to impose restrictions upon consumer credit during inflationary periods or periods of national emergency. During an inflationary period the control of consumer credit restricts the amount of buying and, therefore, exerts a downward pressure on prices.

Moral Suasion. Moral suasion refers to the attempt by monetary authorities of the Federal Reserve (and other key government leaders) to persuade banks, businesses, and consumers to alter their spending practices on moral grounds. Sometimes the process is called simply "jaw-boning." You might wonder how effective this type of monetary control could be. In many countries moral suasion is quite effective. Monetary officials and other government policy makers make recommendations in speeches, public announcements, and various publications suggesting certain activities that they would like to have followed. These suggestions are generally coupled with hints that if the banks, businesses, or consumers do not follow these suggestions, the Fed (or other governmental agencies) will impose drastic restrictions upon them. Since banks, businesses, and consumers are aware of the types of restrictions that can be imposed, they will frequently follow the suggestions of the monetary authorities and government officials on a voluntary basis rather than have the restrictions imposed, and thereby, become compulsory. Commercial bank officials are especially sensitive to suggestions made by central bank officials.

When monetary officials wish to restrict the amount of credit available in an economy, they are following what is called a *tight money policy*. In such a situation, money is difficult to obtain. A tight money policy is followed when the monetary officials wish to curb inflationary tendencies. The process is frequently referred to as "cooling off an overheated economy."

When monetary officials encourage the expansion of credit, they are following what is referred to as an *easy money policy*. An easy money policy is followed at times when productive resources are not being used to their proper capacity and the unemployment level is higher than what is considered tolerable. An easy money policy tends to promote business activity and to stimulate demand.

Combining Monetary and Fiscal Policies

Earlier in this chapter you saw the types of monetary controls that are available for use by central banks. In developed nations all of these controls are used at different times. The mix varies depending upon the economic conditions that exist. There is generally less of a tendency to rely on monetary policy in developing nations than there is in a highly developed economy. The reason for this situation is that the economic "adjustments" needed in developing countries are generally more severe and are better handled through fiscal policy. In more developed economies, "fine tuning" is frequently needed. In such instances, monetary policy is used in conjunction with fiscal policy to regulate the general level of the economic activity of a nation.

Fiscal policy, as you know, refers to the direct results caused by government spending and taxing. Fiscal policy is, therefore, more direct and generally more decisive than monetary policy. Most nations use fiscal policy as their first line of attack in controlling the general economic level of an economy. Monetary policy is used as a supporting device. By way of analogy you might think of fiscal policy as being similar to the transmission of an automobile. Monetary policy might be likened to the accelerator. When a vehicle is in neutral, a movement of the accelerator may create a good deal of noise but it has little to do with the movement of the vehicle. Also, a shift in gears from low to high is more decisive and direct than the movement of the accelerator. In fact, the accelerator is generally manipulated to stay in harmony with the position of the gear shift.

Continuing our analogy with the automobile, rather drastic measures—similar to applying the brakes—are sometimes used during inflationary periods. Examples include price-wage freezes, restricted credit, rationing, and indexing—converting fluctuating money values (such as wages and loans) into "real" values on a yearly basis through the use of a price index. Generally, inflation is more difficult to control through the use of fiscal and monetary policy than is deflation. To emphasize this point in somewhat exaggerated fashion another analogy might be useful. It is easier to pull an object with the string than it is to have the object go in reverse by pushing the string. This is not to say that economic policies used to curb inflation are ineffective. Quite the opposite is true. The measures used tend, however, to be more drastic and more difficult to employ.

The Quantity Theory of Money

About fifty years ago economists created an equation that they called the quantity theory of money. We shall examine this equation and analyze its application to present day economic problems. It is appropriate that we should close our discussion of money (and for that matter the discussion of economics) with an examination of the quantity theory of money. Such an examination will allow us to review many of the concepts presented in this text and also will demonstrate that economics is dynamic.

If we wish to improve our economic lives we must begin by understanding the economy better. In fact, that is what this textbook has been all about. However, as we learn more about the economy, we also learn how to improve our application of economic policy. In the process, certain economic theories and principles are formulated. In time, some of these theories become much more sophisticated. Other theories (or models) are dropped since their application does not prove to be workable. After all, the test of a good theory is whether or not it will work in practice. Therefore, certain theories are dropped over time and replaced by other theories. The quantity theory of money is an especially interesting theory with which to close our discussion, as it involves a theory that (a) was generally accepted by economists over a long period of time, (b) was dropped as an economic theory for a considerable period of time, and (c) was revised in recent years in the light of new economic knowledge. Thus, the quantity theory of money will provide you with an example of an economic theory that has basically remained the same after its revision, but the analysis has changed considerably.

The Equation for the Quantity Theory of Money

Money plays an extremely important part in the economic lives of all of us. Early economists called money a "veil" since they felt that money in itself did not influence economic activity. If you view money simply as an institution created to reflect the "real" exchange of goods and services, then there is a good deal of truth in this observation. Money does in fact *reflect* the productive activity of a society. Nonetheless, money can be used to influence economic activity. You are already familiar with this process through your analysis of fiscal and monetary policies.

The quantity theory of money was formulated at the time before modern fiscal and monetary theory came into existence. Economists observed that there was a direct relationship between the quantity of money in a society and the general price level. This relationship led them to develop the following equation:

$$MV = PT$$

where $M =$ the amount of money in circulation. (Recall that money consists of all currency plus demand deposits.)

$V =$ the velocity of the circulation of money. (Or stated in another way, simply the number of times during any given period of time, such as a year, that an average dollar is used.)

$P =$ the general price level of goods and services in a society.

$T =$ the number of transactions made in a given economy in a period of time such as a year. (Or stated differently, it is simply a measure of the total output of the economy.)

As you look at the equation you will observe that it is remarkably simple. Actually all that it says is that the amount of money available, M, multiplied by the number of times it is spent, V, is equal to the price of an average sale, P, multiplied by the number of sales or transactions, T. Or to make a simple analogy, it is similar to saying that the money that a customer gives a storekeeper for an article purchased is equal to the money the storekeeper receives from the customer.

The "catch" in the equation $MV = PT$ is that there appears to be a causal relationship between money and prices. When the quantity theory of money was first formulated, economists tended to believe that the velocity of circulation, V, and the number of transactions, T, remained relatively fixed. If you were to accept that assumption, there would, of course, be a direct relationship between the of money in circulation, M, and the general price level, P. However, once the theory had been tested in practical economic situations, it became evident that a change in the money supply did not correspond directly to a change in the price level. Historically in the United States the money supply has increased more rapidly than prices. Given evidence of this type, it became obvious that something must have happened to V or to T in the process.

Going back to our example of a customer buying an article from a shopkeeper, there is no reason to assume that if the customer had an additional amount of money that he or she would automatically spend it thereby increasing the amount given to the shopkeeper to purchase the article in question. In fact, it is quite easy to see that a consumer would probably use the additional money to buy an additional article. In this case, there would be an increase in the number of transactions, T, and the price level, P, would stay the same. In fact, this is exactly what tends to happen in an economy. An increase in the money supply does not automatically cause an increase in prices.

To examine what happened to V over the years is a simple process. All you need to do is to take the total output of a nation, the GNP, and divide it by the actual supply of money, that existed for each year. When economists determined V on a year-to-year basis for the last forty years in the United States, it became obvious that the velocity of money fluctuated significantly from time to time. The conclusion was obvious. People do change their rate of spending and V is not a constant figure. It then follows that a change in the money supply, M, will not automatically change the general price level, P.

The next item that needs to be examined to determine the relationship between the money supply, M, and the general price level, P, is to analyze what happens to the total number of transactions, T, over time. When the quantity theory of money was first formulated, it was assumed that the total number of transactions, T, tended to be relatively constant. In the original equation, T referred to *all* transactions, including those for intermediate goods. However, for simplicity it is quite appropriate to define T as representing only those transactions that enter the final output. In this way, P multiplied by T equals the GNP. Or stated simply in equation form: $PT = GNP$.

Monetary and fiscal policies change the amount of money in circulation. The only way that the total output, T, could remain constant is for an economy to be completely stagnant. In such an economy, the total output could not change as a result of monetary and fiscal policies. To understand why this is not the case, a review of the circular flow is in order at this point.

The Circular Flow and the Quantity Theory of Money

The now familiar flow as presented in chapter 4 provides you with an easy tool for analyzing the quantity theory of money in more detail.

To review briefly how a change in the money supply might affect prices, we shall use two examples:

Example 1: A Sluggish Economy. For this example, assume that the economy is suffering from a recession. Not all productive capacities in terms of land, labor, capital, and entrepreneurship are being used to full capacity. Many who would like to work are unable to find jobs. Businesses are unable to sell all their output and, therefore, have cut back on production. Therefore, their plants and their general productive facilities are not fully utilized.

Now assume that money is injected into the circular flow (refer to p. 47). Actually, the money could be injected from any one component of the now familiar equation for GNP: GNP = $C + I + G + F$. Consumers, for any reason you would like to assume, might increase their expenditures by decreasing savings. This would result in an increase in C. Businesses might launch a new investment program, thereby increasing I. The government might undertake a new project, thereby increasing G. Exports might increase relative to imports for any of a host of reasons and, thereby, increase F. It does not matter for our purposes of analysis to identify the source of the injection into the circular flow. What is important is to assume that an injection did, in fact, take place.

Any injection into the circular flow whether it be from C, I, G, or F, must eventually reach the business firm.* When this happens, the revenue received by business firms is greater than their expenditures. Aggregate demand exceeds aggregate supply. From your previous knowledge of this type of situation you already know what will happen. There are two courses of action available to the business firm. It might attempt to raise prices in the hope of increasing its profits. Or it might increase the production of goods and services so that the aggregate supply is in line with the aggregate demand. If a business firm does, in fact, try to increase prices, it might well be forced to lower them again if reasonable competition exists. Other businesses with idle plants and equipment will attempt to employ their unused capacities and undercut the business firm that attempts to raise prices. Consequently, an injection into the circular flow when a sluggish economy exists tends to pull into service unused productive capacities which, in turn, increase output or T.

Example 2: An Overheated Economy. Assume a situation where all of the productive capacities of an economy are in use. All people seeking employment have found work, and land and equipment are fully utilized. In our circular flow diagram this simply means that the business cannot employ any more factors of production even though they might like to do so.

Given the situation of an overheated economy, there is already a strain on prices because the total output, T, cannot be increased. Given this condition, assume that there is an injection of new money into the circular flow. Once again, it is unimportant whether the injection comes about through C, I, G, or F. The newly injected funds will, as in our previous example, eventually reach the business firm. The business firm must react in one of two ways. It will either attempt to raise its prices or employ additional factors of production to increase its output.

---

*In our circular flow analysis recall that we have assumed that *all* production is done by business firms. When, for example, the government produces goods and services, it is acting as a business firm in our example.

However, in this example, there are no additional factors of production to be drawn into service. The only way that business firms can employ additional factors of production is to bid them away from other business firms. Consequently, either prices of the finished products or the returns to factors (such as wages) will increase. The total output, however, cannot increase because we have already assumed the economy to be operating at total capacity. Consequently, when money is injected into an overheated economy it has a direct affect on prices.

We have now come full circle. We can, in turn, see that the quantity theory of money is relevant if one understands the conditions of the economy when it is applied. The reason the quantity theory of money fell into disfavor for a number of years was that economists had assumed a direct relationship between the amount of money in circulation, M, and the general price level, P. This assumption rests on the fact that there must be full employment and the economy must be operating at a full level of capacity. Consequently, we can conclude that an increase in public or private spending will not necessarily result in higher prices. Rather, it might result in a larger output and lower unemployment. We need to examine the status of the economy in each instance.

twelve

Suggested Methods for Teachers

Raymond H. Muessig and Steven L. Miller

Economics is a practical art, like swimming, driving a car, or baking a cake. It is also an intellectual discipline, like philosophy, psychiatry, or history. Someone* once said that those who do not study history are doomed to relive it; it might equally be said that those who don't study economics are doomed to muddle through it the rest of their days. (Robert B. Bangs, *Men, Money, and Markets: An Introduction to Economic Reasoning*)[1]

The economic way of thinking employs such concepts as demand, opportunity cost, marginal effects, and comparative advantage to *order* familiar phenomena. The economist knows very little about the real world that is not better known by businessmen, engineers, and others who make things happen. What he does know is *how things fit together*. The concepts of economics enable us to make better sense out of what we observe and to think more consistently and coherently about a wide range of interrelated phenomena. (Paul Heyne and Thomas Johnson, *Toward Understanding Macro-Economics*)[2]

Introduction

In a recent edition of his *Basic Economics,* Thomas J. Hailstones says:

> Never before has so much interest and excitement been generated in the subject of economics. In the past few years we have experienced a war, full employment, inflation,

---

*George Santayana (1863-1952) observed that "Those who cannot remember the past are condemned to repeat it."

an energy crisis, recession, an oil embargo, voluntary rationing, tax cuts and tax surcharges, price and wage controls, high interest rates, a money crunch, stagflation, massive layoffs, and a host of other ecomonic forces that have affected our daily lives....[3]

The interest and excitement generated in economics of which Hailstones speaks have been apparent to the three authors cooperatively involved in this book. We have observed and taught involved and stimulated elementary and secondary students and teachers who have discovered that economics can be relevant, meaningful, varied, and enjoyable. Hoping to further the cause of economics in general and of economic education in particular, Dr. Warmke has tried to provide enlightened, useful material on the nature of economics in the first eleven chapters of this volume. In this twelfth chapter, we (R. H. Muessig and S. L. Miller) have endeavored to suggest methods that we hope will make social studies education in general and economic education in particular more appealing, worthwhile, challenging, and pleasurable.

Fostering Economic Awareness

Economic phenomena are an important and omnipresent part of our daily lives, and there are a variety of ways in which elementary and secondary teachers can help learners to gain increased economic awareness. For example, many Americans express their preferences, gratifications, frustrations, and the like through the use of serious and funny bumper stickers, a number of which have economic connotations. As a means of stimulating learners in grades four through twelve to be on the lookout for economically oriented bumper stickers that could be shared and discussed in class, the teacher might read aloud to the class selections from *The World's Worst Bumper Stickers,* such as these:

Boycott farmers—Don't eat!

The gas war is over (Gas won)!

The Lord Giveth—Uncle Sam Taketh Away[4]

Then, the teacher could announce to class members that a particular period on a given date would be reserved for them to tell their classmates about economically related bumper stickers they have seen in different places. The following are just a few possibilities:

Live in the past; it's cheaper.
Buy American!
God isn't making more land these days.
Room for one more? Adopt.
Less is better!
Profit is not a dirty word in Ohio!
Save our schools! Vote for the levy!
Massachusetts: Land of Taxes!
God bless farmers!
Visit here, but don't move here!

America can't afford four more years of Carter!
Save gas! Car pool it!
Economize! Fight Bureaucracy!
Don't blame me; I voted Republican!

Depending on the maturity level and the experiential base of students, various general ideas and specific concepts might be identified, clarified, amplified, and exemplified in a classroom exchange. For instance, "Live in the past; it's cheaper." could trigger reactions tied to inflation, and "Buy American!" might launch interaction germane to balance of trade, tariffs, the devaluation of the dollar, and unemployment.

A second methodological recommendation which could foster economic awareness could also increase the economic literacy, vocabulary, of middle, junior high, and senior high school students. First, the class might use a source such as Stanley R. Greenfield's *National Directory of Addresses and Telephone Numbers*,[5] which contains a section listing daily newspapers with circulations of over 50,000. Each learner might select one daily which interests him or her for one reason or another. By state, alphabetically, for example, one person might write to the *News* in Birmingham, Alabama; another individual could communicate with the *Gazette* in Phoenix, Arizona; still another student might contact the *Arkansas Democrat* in Little Rock; a fourth class member could get in touch with the *Examiner* in San Francisco; and so on. Every participant would address a personal letter to the newspaper of his or her choice requesting a complimentary copy of the first page of the paper on a specified date, say a Friday, two weeks from the current date. The envelope containing the letter would also hold a self-addressed, stamped envelope in which the front page could be returned. Each correspondent could receive her or his first page at home so she or he would be able to bring something to school to share with classmates.

Second, with a broad liquid marker, everyone could draw a line around each article on the newspaper's front page that is pertinent to economics in some way. For example, if a given class member were to have received the first page of *The Columbus Dispatch* for 19 April 1978,[6] she or he might put a broad border on the outside of four stories. The streamer story, immediately below the masthead of the paper and running six columns across the entire page about three inches deep, has the headline "U. S. Economic Output Drops First Time in 3 Years." On the same page, there is a four-column story entitled "State Solon Sues To Stop Advance of Funds To Cleveland City Schools." There are also two, two-column stories, "Emergency Gas Buy Ordered 2nd Time" and "Compromise Reached on State Salaries Hike," included on the A-1 page.

Third, still using the first page of the daily, and this time with a narrow liquid marker, the individual learner might underline every word which has economic connotations. Then, each word could be written on a separate 3"× 5" card and the cards arranged in alphabetical order. For instance, the person receiving the 19 April 1978 front page of *The Columbus Dispatch* just cited above might submit these thirty cards:

bond	cash position
business	consumer
buy	cost recovery

curtailment	money
economic indicators	pay-raise
economic output	personal income
economists	property tax levies
economy	purchase
expenditures	recession
exports	retail
financial	revenues
gain	spending
Gross National Product	supplies
inflation rate	unemployment
investments	workers

Fourth, the teacher might form a committee, composed, say, of those class members whose birthdays are closest to the date of the front page of the newspapers being used. The committee would receive the alphabetized stacks of 3"× 5" cards everyone has turned in, locate a room in the school that is not in use, place all of the hundreds of cards in alphabetical order on the floor of the vacant room, eliminate all the duplicate cards, write a master list of the remaining cards in alphabetical order, and print the final vocabulary list on the far left side of sheets of experience chart paper (most frequently used in the primary grades). The sheets of experience chart paper could be mounted on large pieces of poster board and arranged alphabetically along the chalk trays in the classroom.

Fifth, there would be a space for tally marks on the appropriate line to the right of each word, term, concept, etc. Wide liquid markers could be placed at convenient intervals along the chalk trays. Whenever one of the vocabulary list items is used during a class activity, an alert student could quietly leave her or his seat and use the broad felt tip pen to put a tally mark behind the item. In time, perhaps over a period of two to three weeks, the teacher might endeavor to find a way for each of the items to be used by learners in some kind of meaningful context. Through the approach just described, an individual participant could gain additional economic awareness, use and improve vital reading skills, and add to his or her vocabulary.

Making the Concept of Scarcity Increasingly Meaningful

In *Economics: The Way We Choose,* Paul W. Barkley writes, "Economics is the study of the allocation of scarce resources among alternative and competing ends." "In less elegant language," Barkley adds, "economics is the study of how to use what is available to get what is wanted."[7] In *Economics in Society: Concepts and Institutions,* Suzanne Wiggins Helburn, John G. Sperling, Robert G. Evans, and Elizabeth J. Lott define *economics* as "the science which studies how people acting in groups decide to use scarce resources, which have alternative uses, to satisfy their wants." These authors use *scarcity* to mean "a *relative condition* which exists whenever wants are greater than the resources available to satisfy them."[8] In *Economics: An Analysis of Principles and Policies,* Thomas J. Hailstones and Michael J. Brennan observe:

> Without *scarcity* the world would have no economic problems, and there would be no need to study economics. Each member of the human race could enjoy as much of everything as he might conceivably want. Everyone on the planet could have any amount of automobiles, clothes, books, gourmet dinners, pedicures, psychiatric consultations, sauna baths, movies, sporting events, wigs, and so on without end. Of course we do not live in such a fairyland; these goods and services are not superabundant. ... [9]

And, in *Toward Understanding Macro-Economics,* cited previously, Heyne and Johnson explain:

> *If everyone can have all that he wants of some good without being required to sacrifice anything else that is also wanted, that good is not scarce.* It is a *free good.* There are obviously not many free goods available in our society, despite the song that says the best things in life are free. Perhaps the best things in life cannot be purchased with money; but that does not make them free goods.[10]

Not only is scarcity discussed by many economists in textbooks and a variety of other sources, but it is also regarded often as *the* central concept of economics. And, conceptually, one of the especially appealing features of the discipline of economics is the beautiful way in which numerous concepts interrelate. Methodologically, therefore, though the elementary or secondary teacher may focus on scarcity as we have here, it is not possible nor desirable to try to exclude other key ideas, including economic choices, opportunity costs, trade-offs, and the like. As a matter of fact, there are many arguments in favor of integrating economic insights in particular and understandings in various social sciences in general.

Dealing with the concept of scarcity can be easy and gratifying at all instructional levels—including the primary grades as suggested in a following teaching strategy. First, the teacher could explain that each little person is going to have an opportunity to make something for himself or herself, a relative, a friend, a classmate, a pet, etc. The teacher might allocate the same resources—construction materials—to each child in the class, including such items as a pair of blunt primary scissors, a generous glob of paste in a jar lid, three crayons and three sheets of construction paper in different colors, two paper containers for frozen fruit juice concentrate (one 6-ounce and one 12-ounce), and one 16-ounce can with the rough, sharp edges filed away.

Second, the teacher could cover the top of a large table in the front of the classroom with additional construction materials, such as buttons in various shapes, sizes, and colors; pieces of yarn in different plies, lengths, and colors; drinking straws in varied diameters and colors; small, clear polyethylene bags containing variegated sequins; little boxes of decorative stickers (flowers, birds, pets, etc.); and so on. There might be six items for each little girl or boy. (Thus, in a class enrolling 22 children, there would be 132 items displayed on the large table.)

Third, the teacher could invite every pupil to choose six items from the table. The teacher could ask one individual to move from child to child with a shoe box containing slips of paper numbered from 1-22. Each participant would draw a slip from the box. The number on the slip would determine the order in which children would get a turn to select optional construction materials. Using a timer, the teacher could give each class member three minutes in which to make her or his choices of the six items from the table.

Fourth, the teacher might announce that the whole class will have six minutes in which to trade both the original construction materials allocated by the teacher and the six items picked from the table. Since there would be no a priori prices assigned to any of the resources and no official system of currency, boys and girls could barter as they see fit—a can for a bag of sequins, a piece of yarn for a crayon, and so forth.

Fifth, each youngster might have a half hour in which to make one or more products, including such possibilities as pencil holders, playthings for kittens, railroad engines, flower pots, dog collars, Christmas tree ornaments, purses, cars and trucks, paper dolls, bonnets, mobiles, bracelets, and party hats.

Sixth, at the end of the half hour, the classroom might be turned into a "bazaar." The chairs could be moved out of the way, and the desks could be arranged in rows along the edge of the walls of the room, thus permitting "shoppers" to move easily from one "store" to another. Every child's product(s) would be displayed on her or his desk. After everyone has had an opportunity to walk by each desk and to see and appreciate the work of his or her classmates, the teacher might indicate that ten minutes will be set aside for a second round of trading. Unused resources might be exchanged for unused resources; unused resources and products could be traded; and products might be bartered for products.

Seventh, the primary teacher might guide a culminating class discussion focused largely on the concept of scarcity. At their own level of understanding, in their own words, and in whatever order occurs to them, children might contribute observations such as the following:

> The initial resources—construction materials—that class members were allocated limited the kinds and the number of things that could be produced and the trades that could be made for initial resources and items available from the large table.
>
> The supply and variety of items available to everyone on the large table restricted the types and quantity of products that could be made and the exchange possible for initial resources and large-table items.
>
> The small amount of time allowed for picking out items from the large table prevented girls and boys from considering many ways in which the items might be used for production and trading.
>
> There was insufficient time, too, for thinking about the bartering of both the initial resources and the six items.
>
> Also, a half hour was not long enough for the members of the class to come up with their very best ideas for things to make and to turn out products of the highest possible quality.
>
> Much more time was needed as well for the second round of trading.
>
> Although the scarcity of time and materials made the strategy more difficult and frustrating, it also made this approach more challenging and interesting.

Of course, the strategy just described can be readily adapted for use all of the way through the twelfth grade, not only to make the concept of scarcity increasingly meaningful, but also to introduce, reinforce, and enlarge understandings of such concepts as choices, opportunity costs, trade-offs, specialization, division of labor, and supply and demand. At the middle school level, for example, a social studies class might constitute itself as a corporation, with shareholders, officers, employees, and all. Class members could have an opportunity to purchase shares of stock. Students could decide whether there might be 25 shares @ $1 per share, 50 shares @ 50¢ per share, 100 shares @ 25¢ per share, and so on. The group would choose from among various goods it might produce within the limitations (scarcity) imposed by the funds it has from the sale of stocks, looking carefully at opportunity costs and trade-offs involved. Anticipating the approach of spring, for instance, the class might decide to go into the kite business, which would mean that it would have to forego other undertakings that might be more or less profitable. A committee of student purchasing agents might be dispatched to several hobby stores to find out the cost of supplies (e.g., spruce sticks, tissue paper, glue, paint) necessary to manufacture kites. The number of kites that could be constructed from the supplies that $25 would buy would have to be figured out and a possible retail price estimated. Obviously, supply and demand would be a fascinating and vital factor. The retail price per kite *might* be higher on the first day of the kite season than it would be later in the spring. However, a great deal would depend on the number of stores that have kites for sale on the first day of the season, on the retail prices of kites in the stores, and so on. Students might also devote considerable time and thought to the division of labor in class, so that each person does his or her fair share of the work and performs the work most suited to his or her talents. Assuming that the first kites produced sell out quickly, the appeals and drawbacks of mass-producing additional kites could be weighed.

Literature for children and adolescents is an excellent way to motivate and to sustain purposeful class discussions of the concept of scarcity and other worthwhile activities, including book reports, buzz groups, skits, and role-playing sessions. With the help of parents, friends, fellow teachers, instructional media specialists, school and public librarians, centers for economic education, and the like, the elementary or secondary social studies teacher could easily stock a shelf with books pertaining to scarcity, written at various reading levels. In addition to encouraging as much independent reading as possible, the teacher could read aloud to the class from sources such as those identified here.

In all the elementary grades the concept of scarcity and other related economic ideas could be explored through the picture book *Alexander, Who Used to Be Rich Last Sunday*, written by Judith Viorst and illustrated by Ray Cruz. As the teacher reads the story aloud and displays the pictures for the class to see, children could discuss the ways in which Alexander goes through a dollar, with the purchase of bubble gum, losses on bets, the rental of a snake, fines for using "certain words" and for kicking "certain things," acquisitions at a garage sale, and the like. These excerpts capture something of the feeling of the printed matter:

> ...I used to be rich. Last Sunday. Last Sunday Grandma Betty and Grandpa Louie came to visit from New Jersey. They brought a dollar for me...
>
> ...Eddie called me up and said that he would rent me his snake for an hour. I always wanted to rent his snake for an hour.
> Good-bye twelve cents.[11]

Sidewalk Story by Sharon Bell Mathis could be read independently by many pupils in the intermediate grades. Or, the teacher could read the book aloud and invite a consideration of its economic significance. A sensitive, memorable exchange of thoughts and feelings could be inspired by passages such as this:

... I'm all right and I can work. But if I don't work, I don't get any money for that day.... With seven children, somebody is always sick. I can't go to work and leave no sick baby with Tanya. If I'm sick it don't matter, I go to work anyway.... I spend the money first for food and sometimes for medicine. I got too far behind with my rent this time.[12]

Learners in grades five through eight could enjoy listening to and talking about *The Bad Times of Irma Baumlein* by Carol Ryrie Brink. The protagonist is indeed faced with a problem of unlimited wants and limited resources in the following excerpt:

... Ahead of her (Irma Baumlein) saw the toy department, and her heart leaped with hope. It looked as if they had every kind of toy in the world.
Everything was beautifully new and shiny. Toy trains went around shiny tracks, toy airplanes whizzed overhead. There were monster-making sets galore and stuffed tigers, elephants, monkeys, giraffes, and even little dogs that could be wound up and made to jump and bark.
Irma stopped wistfully beside the chemistry sets, but she knew that she would not have enough money left to buy one after she had bought the doll. So she went straight to the doll corner.
There were so many dolls that it made her head whirl. They were all smiling madly with very professional smiles. "Buy me! Buy me!" they seemed to say. "I'm just the one you want."[13]

Abby O'Neill, an eleven-year-old, who has her twelfth birthday later in *Me and Mr. Stenner* by Evan Hunter, is experiencing a real scarcity problem, with which learners in grades five through nine might identify at this point in the story:

My allowance each week was two dollars... I usually spent the money on the following items:
Little glass bottles, which I adored.
Bubble gum, which I similarly adored.
Airmail stamps, to write to Grandmother Lu in California.
I usually got my allowance on Saturday morning. By Saturday afternoon at three o'clock, I had usually *spent* my allowance. So the problem was:
... How could I buy Daddy a Christmas present with allowances I'd already spent?[14]

Just the Beginning by Betty Miles and *Mr. and Mrs. Bo Jo Jones* by Ann Head are among the numerous adolescent novels which could be used to vivify the concept of scarcity and allied personal-social concerns facing secondary students.

... (E)ven though Dad works about ten hours a day at the store, he still doesn't earn very much. Julia's going to college next year and even if she gets a scholarship—I just know she will—she'll need extra money. Dad worries about that. The money Mom makes will help. I think Dad wouldn't mind Mom working if it was work she really liked. But he doesn't want her to have to clean other people's houses. ... Sometimes I just wish we were rich.
I asked Julia, "Did you ever wish we lived in a big house in The Woods and never had to worry about money?"
Julia laughed. "Of course. You know what I'd do the very first thing? Go to a shoe store and buy the exact pair of boots I wanted without even looking at the price tag."
"I'd buy a camel's-hair wrap coat," I said. "And a horse."
We both laughed. ... [15]

... Bo Jo had three hamburgers and a banana split, and I had one hamburger and two chocolate malteds. When we got back in the truck, Bo Jo counted his money. He figured he had enough for gas back to Trilby and eight bucks over. He said, "I'll be back in a minute." There was a florist shop across the street and he went into it. When I saw him come out with a small purple box in his hand, I got a lump in my throat as big as a grapefruit. He put the box on the seat between us, and I opened it. It was a white orchid tied with a white ribbon.

"I would have got it before," he said, "but I had to see how much that marriage merchant was going to charge first."[16]

Examining Choices Necessitated by Scarcity

In *Learning About Why We Must Choose,* a book which might be used as a resource in the intermediate and secondary grades, John E. Maher and S. Stowell Symmes write:

> Choices! Choices! Choices! Economic choices are a basic part of human behavior. We try to make choices that will give us the kind of satisfactions that help to make our lives better.
>
> It is because most goods and services are economically scarce that economic choices must be made. If people could get the things they wanted merely by wishing for them, there would be no need to make economic choices.[17]

Jim Eggert's *What Is Economics?* states that economics is "the science (or art) of making choices—choosing the *best way* to organize and/or combine our limited resources to meet our material needs."[18] The *Master Curriculum Guide in Economics for the Nation's Schools; Part I, A Framework for Teaching Economics: Basic Concepts,* developed by W. Lee Hansen, G. L. Bach, James D. Calderwood, and Phillip Saunders has this to say:

> The overriding characteristic of all productive resources is that these resources are limited relative to human wants, and that adding to them requires the use of additional resources. Consequently, the goods and services that can be produced with these limited resources are themselves limited. These two conditions require that people must continuously make *choices* about how to use the scarce resources available to them.... [19]

And, we might further set the stage for our subtopic devoted to choices by referring to what Professor Warmke has written in the first chapter of this book. *"Economics,"* Warmke states, *"is basically a study of the choice-making process used by individuals and total societies in their attempt to satisfy their needs and wants for goods and services."*

Just as fiction was suggested in the immediately preceding material on scarcity, so it can also be employed nicely with respect to choices. At the primary level, for instance, the teacher might use *Would you rather...,* a delightful children's picture book, written and illustrated by John Burningham. Here is a sample of the textual matter:

Would you rather have...
supper in a castle
breakfast in a balloon
or tea on the river [20]

Another picture book, *Surprise for Mrs. Burns* by Glennette T. Turner, could foster a discussion in grades two and three.

> On their way out of the lunchroom, Vanessa said, "You know, I was just thinking we should give Mrs. Burns something—something she can look at and say, 'My class gave me this.'"
>
> Jackie said, "Hey!... When we gave (a) party for our mother, we got her a gift with trading stamps."
>
> Richard spoke up. "My mother works near the place where you turn in stamps to get stuff. She could get the gift."
>
> "We have a catalog at home that shows all the things you can get with stamps. I'll bring it tomorrow," Vanessa offered.
>
> The children turned page after page, but they couldn't find the right gift.
> Somebody said, "How about a popcorn popper?" and everyone giggled.
> Finally Jackie snapped her fingers and said, "Hey, I know! We could get her a camera—and take pictures of the party." [21]

In grades four through seven, Beverly Cleary's *Henry Huggins* offers possibilities for independent reading and for total class involvement concerning choices with excerpts such as these:

> "I brought you a lot of guppies," Henry said to Mr. Pennycuff. "I hope you can use them."
>
> "Use them!" exclaimed Mr. Pennycuff. "I certainly can. I haven't had a guppy in this store since the sale. Let's see them."
>
> "Well, now," said Mr. Pennycuff, "I guess these fish are worth about seven dollars. I can't give it to you in money, but you can pick out seven dollars' worth of anything in the store you want."
>
> Seven dollars! Henry was astounded. Seven dollars' worth of anything in the pet shop! He was rich!...
>
> "Take anything you want, sonny. Dog collars, kittens, bird seed. Anything."
> Henry tried to decide what he would like.... [22]

Middle, junior high, and high school students would likely be intrigued considerably and touched deeply by the tremendously important economic choices identified in *Hey, Big Spender!* by Frank Bonham.

> "According to my lawyer, Gideon Jordon," said Breathing Man, "I am one of the richest black men who ever lived, not counting black emperors, musicians, fighters, and such."
>
> "... Long as I swings to my own tune, I'm all right. Eat simple food. Drink one beer a day, usually. Tend to my breathing. And the mostliest thing—don't get excited."

"Now, how'm I going to do all them things if I let people know I just inherited a half-million dollars?"

"I made (my lawyer) swear not to tell *nobody* about this. Because the first reporter who came around to interview me, I'd be *dead* (from exciting a weak heart) right then. So I told Jordon I was going to give it all away."

"And (this) hundred (is) the first you're giving away? Man, that's real fine. My aunt will—"

"No, no—that's your first week's salary. *You're* going to give it away."

"You're going to front for me. Talk to people who need money. Help me decide who gets it."

... "You know how old I am?" (Walter ("Cool") Hankins) said. "Just turning eighteen. And strictly speaking, I don't know Thing One about much of anything. ..."

"You know all you need to. You know what hurts. You know *who* hurts. You know this town is full of people just *dying* of their hurts. And money would help most of them. So you'll talk to them, find out where they hurt, how much they need—"

... "You're going to rent a little store-front office. Put up a sign: FREE MONEY. HOPE OFFICE. People will come and tell you what they need. You're gonna write the high points down on cards. At night you bring them here. And we pick a winner."[23]

In the context of an American history, an economics, a senior problems, or some other such class, the senior high school teacher could make excellent use of *No Promises in the Wind* by Irene Hunt, a novel concerning the Great Depression and the limited economic choices which confronted many people.

... My paper route didn't mean much money, but it was important. Dad had been out of work for eight months, and only the day before, my sister had received notice of a cut-back in personnel which cost her the clerking job she'd had for nearly a year. Every few pennies counted in our family...

... There he sat in the midst of dirt and trash, and directly in front of him was a lean alley cat which he stroked as it lapped milk from a rusty pan. A five-cent milk bottle was in Joey's hand.

"She was just about starved, Josh," he said quickly as if realizing that he must come up with an explanation. Joey knew well enough that milk was not for alley cats that fall. "She's got babies, and she needs milk awful bad. You're not mad at me, are you?"

"Where did you get a nickel for milk?" I asked sternly.

"Kitty gave it to me. She walked home from the elevated yesterday to save streetcar fare, and she gave me the nickel because she couldn't buy me a present for my birthday last week. It was *my* nickel, Josh, honest. And the mother cat was so hungry."

"Kitty's in big business giving you a nickel when she's just been laid off her job," I answered. "And you listen to me, Joey—when you get hold of a nickel, you give it to mom to help with groceries. I don't know what Dad would do to you if he knew you'd bought milk for a mangy alley cat."

... I was making Joey feel that he had committed a crime in being compassionate. Once I had been as eager as he was to feed every stray animal that came near us. It was strange what poverty and fear of hunger could do to a sense of decency.[24]

A second basic teaching strategy which might facilitate an examination of choices necessitated by scarcity could be modified handily for use in grades six through eleven. However, the illustration provided here is suggested for use with high school seniors. This approach encourages twelfth graders to think about the possible short- and long-range consequences of economic choices, and, to the imaginative classroom teacher, it should suggest a natural tie-in with opportunity costs and trade-offs.

First, in a session involving the entire class, the teacher could ask the seniors to think of as many goods and services as possible which they might need and want following their graduation from high school. As students suggest possibilities, the teacher could list on the chalkboard items such as a trip (Florida, Alaska, England, Europe, Africa), athletic equipment (jogging shoes, baseball glove, skis, golf clubs), appliances (electric frying pan, toaster, range, washer), insurance (automobile, theft, fire, life), sound equipment (radio, amplifier, turntable, tape player, speakers), contact lenses, tools, a used or new motorcycle, car, tractor, or boat, tuition (trade school, business school, technical institute, junior college, college, university), luggage, a pet, dance lessons, a new wardrobe, furniture, and/or an engagement ring.

Second, each individual in the class could be requested to come up with a specific, confidential, expendable sum of money, based on such sources as past savings, possible monetary graduation gifts, anticipated net earnings the year after graduation, etc.

Third, every class member could write each of the goods and services she or he needs and wants on a separate 3"× 5" card, disregarding the funds that may be available. At this stage of the teaching strategy, participants might require two or three days for independent research in class, during study halls, and after school. By asking relatives, friends, classmates, teachers, and others, telephoning, shopping, checking in catalogs, reading advertisements, and so on, the student-researcher would arrive at an approximate price for each good and service needed and wanted. The price would be written under the appropriate item on every one of the individual 3"× 5" cards.

Fourth, the teacher might give the students directions such as these:

> *Please go through your cards slowly and carefully and think about each good or service you need or want. Now, choose the cards representing the needs and wants you would like very much to satisfy as soon as possible.*
>
> *All right? Next, please stack your cards. On the top, put the card which has on it the good or service you could and/or would like to have first. The next card from the top of your pile should be your second choice, and so on, until you have ranked all of your cards.*
>
> *Here are four sheets of lined paper stapled in the upper left-hand corner. (A set of four lined pages would be distributed to everyone in the class.) Please write your name in the upper right-hand corner of the first sheet. On the top line of the first sheet of paper, next to the left-hand margin line, write the approximate price you have on the card for your first choice. Turn the first card face down. Write the price you have on the second card just under the first price on the first lined sheet of paper. Add the two prices. For example, if your first choice might cost $50, and your second choice might cost $100, you would have a total of $150 on the third line. Turn the second card face down, and so on. Keep doing this, until you have 'spent' all the money you figured that you might have*

from past savings, graduation gifts, net earnings the year after graduation, and the like.

Fifth, the social studies teacher might assist the entire group of twelfth graders in working out a down-to-earth definition of "short-range consequences." Using words such as *now, today, right away, at this time, presently, shortly, soon,* and *in the near future,* the teacher could help students to build an understanding that the short-range consequences of money spent on a good or service are the more immediate pay-offs, results, effects, satisfactions gained—as differentiated from deferred gratifications. As soon as participants have the idea, the teacher could ask each person to take the top-ranked cards for which early satisfaction was sought and for which available funds were "spent," and to write on the second lined sheet in the stapled set a paragraph or two on the possible short-range consequences of the choices made.

Sixth, the teacher might provide the class with a new set of instructions similar to the following:

Would each of you please return to her or his 3"× 5" cards? Put all of your cards face up, and shuffle them thoroughly. You have just learned something about short-range consequences, right? Now, will you please think about long-range consequences? This second time, choose the cards representing needs and wants you would like very much to satisfy in the future for which you are willing to give up goods and services in the present. Next, stack your cards. On the top, put the card which has on it the good or service so important to you that you are willing to wait for it the longest. You care so much about having this really important good or service in the future that you will do without a number of other things in the present and the near future. Got it? Good. The next card from the top of your pile should be your second long-range choice, and so on, until you have ranked all of your cards.

On the top line of the first sheet of paper in your stapled set, over on the far right side, write the approximate price you have on the card for your first choice. Turn the first card face down. Write the price you have on the second card just under the first price on the right side of the first lined sheet of paper. Add the two prices. Turn the second card face down, and so on. Keep doing this, until you have 'spent' all of the money you figured that you might have.

Seventh, the teacher might guide the class toward a useful definition of "long-range consequences." Employing words such as *later, after awhile, in a few years, eventually, in time, someday,* and *in the future,* the teacher could help learners to understand that the long-range consequences of money spent on a good or service are the delayed, deferred gratifications—as distinguished from the more immediate results and satisfactions. As soon as the seniors have the idea, the teacher could ask each person to take the top-ranked cards for which future gratification was sought and for which available funds were "spent," and to write on the third lined sheet in the stapled set a paragraph or two on the possible long-range consequences of the choices made.

Eighth, the social studies teacher could offer still another set of instructions, such as these:

> *You are doing beautifully! I think you are ready to tackle what may be the hardest part of this whole strategy, which I developed to encourage you to think reflectively about the possible consequences of economic choices made necessary because of scarcity.*
>
> *Would each of you return a third time to his or her 3"× 5" cards, please? Put all of your cards face up and shuffle them again. You have learned something about short-range consequences and long-range consequences. This is a good time for you to think about both short- and long-range consequences and waves of consequences somewhere in between. Here's your chance to "compromise," "give and take a little, "split some differences," "steer the in-between course," "try the middle way," or whatever you would like to call it. This third time, choose the cards representing needs and wants for goods and services that you would like to safisfy as soon as possible, along the way, and sometime in the future. Next, stack your cards, mixing your short-, middle-, and long-range choices according to your beliefs. Next, stack your cards. On the top, put the card which has on it the good or service most important to you for various reasons, whether you would like to have this good or service right away, before too long, or quite awhile from now. The next card from the top of your pile should be your second preference, though the 'why' and the 'when' for this selection could be different from that of the first card. Continue until you have ranked all of your cards.*
>
> *In the middle, on the top line of the first sheet of paper in your stapled set, write the approximate price you have on the card for your first choice. Turn the first card face down. Write the price you have on the second card just under the first price in the middle of the first lined sheet of paper. Add the two prices. Turn the second card face down, and so on. Keep doing this, until you have 'spent' all of the money you figured you might have.*

Ninth, the teacher could ask every individual to take the last set of top-ranked cards for which available funds were "spent," and to write on the fourth lined sheet in the stapled set a paragraph or two or three on the possible short-, middle-, and long-range consequences of the choices made.

Tenth, the teacher might lead a class discussion in which the seniors could share some of the insights gained from the teaching strategy, such as the following:

> *On one of my cards, I had a trip to Florida, just to soak up some sun. I wanted to do that right after I graduated. I decided that the Florida economic choice had mostly short-range consequences tied to it, unless—you know, I mean—I got so much sun that I might have skin cancer years later, or the money I spent might somehow change my whole life somehow. Anyway, the Florida thing got ranked the first time we did this. OK?*
>
> *On another card, I had sound equipment. I thought that a year or two after I got out of college I would get a really good tuner, amplifier, tape player, and set of speakers. I figured sound equipment would have good long-range consequences. I mean, I could enjoy listening to good music for years, right? So, the sound equipment was rated in our second round.*

Well, the third, compromise session, I came up with a brilliant idea! I'd give up the Florida tan, which would disappear before long anyway. I would put aside the money I might have spent on Florida. I'd do without some other things on my first list. I'd ask around at stores and look in display and classified ads. I'd see if I could find some pretty good, new sound equipment on sale, or I'd check into better, used stuff somebody was willing to sell for a fair price. I would be giving up some short-range things I wanted. I would settle for sound equipment that would cost a lot less than what I had in mind for a long time from now. I'd compromise and enjoy the long-range consequences of nice music beginning soon and lasting for a number of years. What do you think!?

I had the hots for a new car, as soon after graduation as possible. I looked into this from a bunch of angles. A new car and all the stuff it involved—interest, insurance, gas, oil changes and lube jobs, tune-ups, repairs, replacement tires and parts, and other jazz—took up my whole first list and then some! You know, a car really cuts out a lot of other choices! After using most of my savings for a down payment, and figuring on a five-year loan—if I could get that big a loan at my age and talk my parents into going along and all—, I would have to come up with about $300 a month to own and drive a new car! Scary, isn't it?! In five years—sort of looking at the long-range consequences of something I wanted right away for a lot of reasons—, a new car wouldn't be worth much; I'd lose most of the new-car price in depreciation. Well, you're getting the idea, aren't you?

OK I want to go to college a lot. That goal was right up there on my second list. I've thought about a bunch of the long-range consequences of getting a college degree, and I believe that most of the possible results are good ones...for me, anyway.

Now, I'm on my third list. I gave up the idea of a new car. I thought about a used car as one of my compromises right away, of course, but I decided against even a used car. My dad says that when you buy a used car, you buy another person's problems. I didn't give up the college thing, but I had to make a compromise from my second list to my third—a compromise I'd been kicking around in my brain for awhile anyway. I wanted to go to a small, private college in another city, but the costs for tuition and for room and board were just too much, especially for the whole four years. So, I'll live at home, attend the branch of the state university here in our town the first two years, work part-time during the regular school year and full-time in the summer, save as much money as I can, and then go to the main branch of the state university the last two years... or, maybe, even the small college. Oh, yeah, the branch of the state university is about two miles or so from my house, and the bus service isn't all that hot. So, an item toward the bottom of my third list is a ten-speed bicycle. I hope some of you will let me mooch rides from time to time and ask my date and me on double dates! But, really, my folks are pretty good about letting me borrow the family wheels.

I'm glad we did this. I found out that I have a lot of choices and that what you choose makes a difference right away and later.

Helping Learners Understand Specialization

Forced into making choices as we are by scarcity, we could widen our range of choices if there were a way to reduce scarcity somewhat.

Getting more output from our limited resources is one way of alleviating (but not eliminating) the basic economic fact of scarcity. Choices are still inevitable, but they are often less painful if productivity is increasing. In addition to getting more output from the same input, increasing productivity can be used to get the same output with less input, thus permitting conservation of limited resources.[25]

Productivity, expressed in a ratio, is "the fraction showing the amount of output per unit of input for some production process. It is used to compare efficiency of two or more production methods.[26]

$$\frac{\text{OUTPUTS}}{\text{INPUTS}} = \text{Productivity Ratio}$$

If a farmer through astute crop rotation is able to grow 15,000 bushels of corn on 50 acres where he used to grow 13,350, the productivity of one acre of land leaps *from 267* [13,350 bushesl/50 acres] to 300 [15,000 bushels/50 acres]. As a result, all of us have more food than we had before without using more resources to get it.

What are some of the ways in which an economy can boost productivity? According to the Office of Economic Research of the New York Stock Exchange, productivity increases when:

— People are better trained, educated and motivated;
— People have better working environments;
— People are in better health;
— People have more efficient machinery and equipment to work with;
— People develop new products and technology;
— People shift from working in less efficient industries to working in more efficient industries;
— People manage more effectively.

In short, productivity increases primarily when people work smarter (sic) and more efficiently.[27]

In the first chapter of this book, Professor Warmke points out that *specialization*, a principle that embodies several of the ideas above, is an important source of increased productivity. He defines specialization as "assigning one person to the performance of a particular task rather than to have one person complete an entire process.... Specialization is also sometimes called *division of labor.*"

Activities to teach students about specialization can be active and participatory as this strategy for intermediate students shows. First, the teacher might explain that each pupil is going into the valentine card business. Each learner could choose his or her company's name, e.g., The Cupid Card Company or Happy Heart Valentines. The teacher could prepare forms on which students would keep their production and expense records. The teacher might work through a sample record by displaying the following form on an overhead transparency.

Suggested Methods for Teachers

COMPANY NAME: <u>VALENTINES UNLIMITED</u>   OWNER: <u>SUSIE HART</u>

	Number of Cards Made	Cost of Materials (20¢/card)	Cost of Equipment (30¢/day)	My Wages ($1.00/day)	Total Expenses (Add all expenses for the day)	Average Cost for Each Card (Total expenses divided by number of cards)
DAY 1	3	$.60	$.30	$1.00	$1.90	$.63
DAY 2	2	.40	.30	1.00	1.70	.85
DAY 3	3	.60	.30	1.00	1.90	.63
TOTAL	8	$1.60	$.90	$3.00	$5.50	$.69

The instructions to the class might proceed something like this:

Susie Hart's company is called Valentines Unlimited. On the first day she made three cards. Each card that she produces has 20 cents worth of materials in it—paper, glue, and so forth. Susie also must rent her work space, her desk, and equipment, her crayons and scissors. That costs 30 cents each day. She must pay herself a wage of one dollar each day as well. If we add up all of her expenses on that day we get $1.90. Now if we divide her total expenses by the number of cards she made, that's $1.90 divided by 3, we get 63 cents. That's called the average cost of each card. Any questions? Now you are to produce only one kind of card. Once you have decided what you like, you are to stick to that design.

Perhaps the teacher might leave the remainder of the transparency blank so that the class can supply the answers to provide feedback on pupil understanding.

Second, the teacher could ask the children to list on the chalkboard the various production steps in making the cards. A design must be created, materials selected, a sketch made, paper cut and folded, valentines lettered, and so forth. On a large table, the teacher might display the materials available for use—a variety of construction paper, glue, scissors, crayons, pastel chalk, tissue paper, pencils, and erasers.

The day before production is to begin, students should make the designs for their cards so that they can begin producing immediately the next day. Production time of perhaps an hour could be set aside each day for three days. Time should be allotted for keeping records of the production. At the end of the production phase, students might exchange records to check for completeness and accuracy. These records should be saved and a sample valentine attached to each.

Fourth, the teacher might explain that the class is about to begin a new kind of valentine card production with new companies. After dividing the class into groups of either four or five, he or she could display a new record form, giving the following directions:

Each group represents a new company. Each person in the company has a special job to do. In a little while you will have a chance to decide which job each person will perform. You will need a manager. The manager's duties include keeping records, making sure that the company has the right materials, filling in for an absent worker at any job, and helping any worker who falls behind in his or her work. In this example, Susie Hart is the manager. What is her job? Good! The cutters cut and fold the card paper and cut out any other design that must be glued to the card. As you see, I have left the cutter job blank on this form. I did that because some companies of four students will not have a cutter. The manager will help the gluer do the cutting and folding. In this example, Elmer Borden is the gluer and his main job will be to glue the cut designs on cards. The writers will be the ones who letter the valentines with whatever message you have selected.

COMPANY NAME: ALL-STAR CARD COMPANY   MANAGER: SUSIE HART
                                         WRITER: VICKY PENN
                                         WRITER: CHUCK SCHULTZ
                                         GLUER: ELMER BORDEN
                                         CUTTER: _____

	Number of Cards	Cost of Materials (20¢/card)	Cost of Equipment (50¢/day)	Wages ($1.00/day/worker)	Total Expenses (Add all expenses for the day)	Average Cost for Each Card (Total expenses divided by number of cards)
DAY 1	16	$3.20	$.50	$4.00	$7.70	$.48
DAY 2						
DAY 3						
TOTAL						

Let's look at this new record form. The first part is the same, number of valentines made on that day, 16. Cost of materials per card, 20 cents, times 16 cards equals $3.20. But the cost of equipment is higher, 50 cents per day. You have a bigger company so you need more space. And all of your workers get $1.00 per day so that's $4.00 for this company. How much would it be if they had a cutter? Right, $5.00. The rest is the same as before. There's a column for total expenses and one for average cost. How do we get that? Very good. At the end of three days we will total just as before. Any questions?

The teacher could point out that each company wants to produce as many cards as possible while emphasizing that "neatness counts." Any sloppily done cards will be "recalled." Displaying all of the various cards produced earlier, the teacher invites the companies to choose which card they will produce. At the end of three days of production, companies could exchange records for an "audit" to check accuracy and completeness.

Finally, the teacher might begin the debriefing phase by comparing the average cost per card of each company when labor was divided among students with that of the company that produced the same card when production was carried on individually. This provides an "apples to apples" comparison since some valentines might be more difficult to make. Each group could report to the class on its comparison.

The teacher could prepare a survey based on Professor Warmke's advantages and disadvantages of specialization. Were the cards of equal quality under specialized production? Did students like making the whole card or specializing in one job? Why? Were some jobs harder than others? Were average costs lower? Why?

The teacher might also be able to arrange a field trip to a local factory where students could see specialization in practice. Students might interview the plant manager or workers, asking some of the questions on their surveys.

The teacher could also ask students to speculate on the effects of specialization on the price that might be charged for the valentines. During this exercise, students could conclude that specialization "helps things cost less" or that it "helps fight inflation." The discussion could easily continue on to related topics such as the nature of productivity, other ways to increase it, supply, and effective management. Thus, there are a variety of fruitful directions to pursue.

Having Fun with the Concept of Interdependence

Specialization refers to more than division of labor on an assembly line. Most workers specialize to some extent—teachers, insurance brokers, accountants—with the result that few people are self-sufficient, or even nearly so. The concomitant interdependence, the reliance on so many frequently unknown others, is an important aspect of the modern economic world. It escapes our attention until some gear in the machinery stops functioning, as when truckers, dock workers, and miners strike, or when short gasoline supplies create long lines at the pumps.

Primary grade children can begin to appreciate the complex web of interdependence and have fun, too, as suggested in the following teaching strategy. The teacher might begin by explaining to children that they are going to pretend that they are all grown-up and that each one has a job. The jobs that the pupils pretend to have are not really the jobs that they will have when they grow up. Next, the teacher could have printed on the chalkboard a list of occupations with which the learners are likely to be familiar. (Many primary teachers present lessons on "community helpers" which could easily serve as the springboard for this lesson.)

Some possibilities are:

Teacher	Doctor
Dentist	Nurse
Letter Carrier	Police Officer
Firefighter	Farmer
Sales Clerk	Pilot
Telephone Operator	Construction Worker

Newscaster	Truck Driver
Bus Driver	Minister/Priest/Rabbi
Railroad Engineer	Secretary
Waiter/Waitress	Principal

The same occupations could be written on slips of paper placed in a coffee can on the teacher's desk. One at a time, each child would draw a slip. Since the pupils might not be able to read the name of the occupation, each one could first whisper his or her guess to the teacher who could whisper back the correct answer if the guess proved to be wrong. Fourth, the child could print his or her name on the board next to the pretend job and invite the class to guess what he or she does in that job. (This spares any unfortunate little person who happens to select an occupation unknown to him or her.)

Fifth, after each child has selected a job, the teacher could instruct class members to draw pictures of themselves in their make-believe jobs. An example or two might be helpful for the pupils. The teacher could display a hand drawn picture of a farmer in broad-brimmed hat astride a tractor in a field. Another drawing might show a bus driver visible through the window of a big, bright, yellow school bus. The teacher could emphasize that the children's drawings should clearly show the workers and identify their jobs by attire, tools, or context.

After the children have completed their pictures, the class could use masking tape to attach the drawings to the largest blank wall in the room, taking care to leave ample space between each illustration. The teacher might then give the following instructions:

> *We now have all of your pictures up on the wall. And they are very nice. Here's Vicki. She's a dentist. See the patient with his mouth wide open. And here's Jay on his fire truck. Is that house on the left on fire, Jay? I see. Good.*
>
> *Now what I would like you to do is to help me decide which of you might need help from someone else. And to do that we will connect pictures with this red ribbon. Let me show you. Here's Steve, the farmer. See him on his tractor? He might need help from Colleen, the truck driver, to haul his crops to market. So we connect Steve with Colleen. Also Sue, the police officer—see her uniform and gun—eats doesn't she? Well, she needs the farmer, so we connect Sue and Steve.*
>
> *Now when I call on you, tell me who you think should be connected and why. Raise your hands. One at a time. Yes, Bud?*

Although each picture could be connected with every other one, this part of the exercise can be concluded when each drawing has five or six connections to other drawings. By carefully guiding the discussion, the teacher can ensure that this will be the case.

The class might further examine interdependence by eliminating pictures one at a time to signify the loss of the goods or services of that job. The children could then trace the ribbons back to the remainng pictures and discribe what effects the loss will have. For example, when the farmer is removed, the truck driver loses her customer and the police officer loses her food source. Each child could focus on what would happen to him or her when the jobs on which they depend are removed. Who would provide food, transportation, protection, etc.? Each one could also examine the effect of the removal of his or her job on the others with whom he or she is connected.

Next, the children should be encouraged to summarize their conclusions. It is not necessary for pupils to be exposed to the term *interdependence* since it is the concept which is of prime importance. A few possible student summaries might be those listed below:

"Everybody needs lots of things."
"Lots of people do stuff for other people."
"I like my pretend job 'cause everybody needed my help."
"I found out I'd be in trouble if some jobs weren't there."
"Lots of jobs are connected with lots of others."
"The wall looks like a spider web with all the jobs being connected and stuff."

Finally, the teacher might lead the discussion back to specialization by examining why people need help from each other.

Providing Opportunities for Students to Investigate Value Questions and Economic Goals

In the *New World of Economics,* Rich McKenzie and Gordon Tullock write, "The approach of the economist is amoral. Economics is not so much concerned with what *should be,* or how individuals should behave, as it is with understanding why people behave the way they do. [28] However, in the consideration of policy questions, related to how our society should solve particular problems, values are inevitably part of the decision-making process. As Peter Kennedy puts it in *Macroeconomics:*

> *Positive economics* is concerned with what *is:* for example, when the government enacts a policy, positive economics analyzes what happens in the economy in response to enacting this policy. *Normative economics* takes as a starting point the results of positive economics and is concerned with what ought to be: for instance, with whether or not the results of a certain policy are desirable. It is important to isolate value judgments so that persons responsible for making them (generally, politicians) can make decisions free of complications associated with positive economics.[29]

Jim Eggert, in *What Is Economics?* connects policy issues with goals. " ... (W)e could say that economics is the study of how we solve economic problems. Conversely, we could say that economics is the study of goals, i.e., how we move closer to economic objectives."[30]

In chapter 2, Dr. Warmke elaborates on economic goals:

> People in most countries generally agree that a nation should strive for economic (1) freedom, (2) efficiency, (3) growth, (4) stability, (5) justice, and (6) security.

The Joint Council on Economic Education's (JCEE) basic curriculum document, *A Framework for Teaching Economics: Basic Concepts,*[31] lists the following goals:

1. Freedom
2. Economic Efficiency

3. Equity
4. Full Employment
5. Price Stability
6. Security
7. Growth

The JCEE document emphasizes decision making, which is the connection between social studies education and values, goals, policy issues, and normative economics:

> High school graduates, as well as college graduates, will be exposed continuously over their lifetimes to a wide variety of economic questions. This will occur through their reading of newspapers and newsmagazaines, their exposure to radio and television, their involvement in political campaigns and civic issues, and their participation in economic life as employees, employers, consumers, union members, and the like. The conclusions they reach on these issues will be reflected in how they vote; in the actions they take as members of unions, civic organizations and businesses; in their responses to appeals by the President and other public officials; and in economic decisions they make as individual consumers, workers, producers, savers and investors. This means that the quality of individual decision-making is crucial to the effective operation of our social system and to the well-being of the individual.
>
> Our purpose is to help to develop in young people, by the time they graduate from high school, an ability to understand and make reasoned judgments about major economic questions facing society and themselves as members of that society. Only in this way can they be responsible citizens and effective decision-makers.[32]

The challenge for the social studies teacher is to help students begin to apply economic tools to decisions about policy issues while recognizing that these choices imply embracing a set of goals which are themselves based upon a complex of values.

One fascinating way to stimulate both student interest in and serious discussion of value issues and economic goals is through the use of rock music. While the bulk of contemporary music seems to center on affairs of the heart frequently described in meticulous detail to a disco beat, a surprising number of writers focus on more weighty matters, including commentary on economic goals. Music can often put in more human terms the urgent need to strive to fulfill society's objectives. Consider the following excerpts from Holly Near's commentary on unemployment in "Laid Off."

"Laid Off"
One dollar left? You may as well buy a beer ... it
    won't buy shoes."
Chorus:
My man's been laid off got trouble, got trouble
My man's been laid off got trouble tonight
First he'll want to talk about it
Then he'll want to fight
Then he'll want to make love to me all night
My man's been laid off got trouble, got trouble
My man's been laid off got trouble tonight

How come I got the trouble?

You know we need the money, you know we need it bad
The money that he's drinking is the last that we had
To do the feeding, feeding, the kids need clothes
They need feeding, feeding, payment on the loan[33]

The song "Laid Off" (lyrics by Holly Near) could be used to launch an investigation into unemployment—personal and social costs of unemployment, unemployment statistics, reasons why unemployment occurs, government compensation programs, and policy choices to remedy the problem.

Achieving economic security has proved a frustrating problem for our society due in no small way to persistent poverty. Stevie Wonder eloquently describes poverty as he sees it in "Village Ghetto Land."

"Village Ghetto Land"

Would you like to go with me
Down my dead end street
Would you like to come with me
To Village Ghetto Land

See the people lock their doors
While robbers laugh and steal
Beggars watch and eat their meals—from garbage cans

Broken glass is everywhere
It's a bloody scene
Killing plagues the citizens
Unless they own police

Children play with rusted cars
Sores cover their hands
Politicians laugh and drink—drunk to all demands

Families buying dog food now
Starvation roams the streets
Babies die before they're born
Infected by the grief

Now some folks say that we should be
Glad for what we have
Tell me would you be happy in Village Ghetto Land[34]

This song (lyrics by Stevie Wonder and Shatema Byrd) opens a variety of topics for further investigation. Is the song an accurate description of ghetto life? How many people are in poverty? Where do they live? Who are the poor? Old? Young? White? Black? What government programs exist to address this problem and have they been at all successful? How much do such programs cost? Are the programs worth the cost? Do the programs deal with symptoms or causes? What alternative solutions have been proposed?

With both songs, the students could examine the value positions the writer seems to adopt and the relation of these values to our economic goals.

Suggested Methods for Teachers

Unfortunately for humankind, the cost of efforts to attain one goal frequently is greater difficulty in realizing another goal. "It is often impossible to achieve all policy goals simultaneously. Attaining one goal can prevent us from attaining another. (Economic) theory permits us to identify the underlying conflict and to describe precisely what 'trade-off' exists between policy goals. . . ."[35]

Music can be used effectively to introduce students to the need to trade-off one goal for another, as described in the following procedure: First, the teacher might secure recordings of "Banquet" by Joni Mitchell and "Show Biz Kids" by Steely Dan and prepare to play the recordings for the class. This requires checking with the media center at the school to determine what equipment is available. For more than one "cut," cassette or reel-to-reel playback is more convenient than changing records. The teachers could prepare an overhead transparency of song lyrics which are usually printed on the album jacket or cover sleeve. (Teachers, following this procedure should be aware of the most recent copyright laws and the possible need to secure written permission to tape music or reproduce lyrics.)

"Banquet"

(Lyrics by Joni Mitchell)
Copyright © 1972 by Crazy Crow Music.

Who let the greedy in
And who left the needy out
Who made this salty soup
Tell him we're very hungry now
For a sweeter fare
In the cookie I read
"Some get the gravy
And some get the gristle
Some get the marrow bone
And some get nothing
Though there's plenty to spare"[36]

"Show Biz Kids"

(Lyrics by W. Becker and D. Fagen)

CHORUS:
While the poor people sleepin'
With the shade on the light
While the poor people sleepin'
All the stars come out at night
They got the house on the corner
With the rug inside
They got the booze they need
All that money can buy
They got the shapely bods
They got the Steely Dan T-shirt
And for the coup-de-gras
They're outrageous

Show biz kids making movies
Of themselves you know they
Don't give a *!#? about anybody else[37]

Second, after providing students with copies of the list of economic goals and definitions published on pages 25-26 of *A Framework for Teaching Economics,* [38] the teacher could play the recordings and display (on an overhead projector) the song lyrics.

Third, students could write a sentence or two describing what the writer's message seemed to be and what value(s) he or she seemed to be advocating. The students could then examine the list of economic goals and accompanying definitions to identify any that may embody the value(s) expressed in the song. For example, students may decide that the songs decry inequitable income between groups. They may identify security or equity as goals which are related.

Next, the teacher might ask what kind of solution could be implemented to address the situation identified in the music. One possible student response could be that income should be redistributed from richer to poorer by taxation and welfare. The class could then explore how such a program might work to the disadvantage of other goals such as freedom, growth, and efficiency. Economic incentives, profits, investment, risk, and markets are examples of economic concepts that could be applied as part of this investigation. Ultimately, students should come to the realization that goals are frequently in conflict and that trade-offs may be necessary.

Music can be used to begin investigating the conflict between economic goals and other social concerns. To explore this, the teacher may ask committees of students to locate examples of songs that argue that economic goals are in conflict with some other important values. The committees could prepare transparencies of the song lyrics for presentation to the class at an assigned time. (Again, the teacher should be aware of the most recent copyright laws and the possible need to secure permission to reproduce lyrics in this manner.) One group may have focused on the apparent conflict between economic growth and environmental issues as presented in the following song:

"Big Yellow Taxi"

(Lyrics by Joni Mitchell)
Copyright © 1970 by Siquomb Publishing Corp.

They paved paradise
And put up a parking lot
With a pink hotel, a boutique
And a swinging hot spot
Don't it always seem to go
That you don't know what you've got
Till it's gone
They paved paradise
And put up a parking lot.

They took all the trees
And put them in a tree museum
And they charged all the people
A dollar and a half just to see 'em
Don't it always seem to go
That you don't know what you've got
Till it's gone
They paved paradise
And put up a parking lot.

Hey farmer farmer
Put away that D.D.T. now
Give me spots on my apples
But leave me the birds and the bees
Please!
Don't it always seem to go
That you don't know what you've got
Till it's gone
They paved paradise
And put up a parking lot.[39]

The group could also be assigned the task of investigating the clash raised in the song. Some members could list what other economic goals may be in conflict with environmental concerns. They might explore the effect of government regulation on price stability and employment, as well as growth. Other students could examine how environmental damage may be related to health problems and worker safety. The teacher might ask the students to list on 3"× 5" cards the value statement, an argument supporting that statement, and any evidence which was gathered to support the policy to which the value applied.

Ultimately, it is the choices we make in society that are the proof of our economic understanding and the goals we support. Thus, students might also bring in recordings of proposed solutions to problems. Some songs advocate revolution, for example:

"Burn Down The Mission"

(Lyrics by Elton John and Bernie Taupin)

You tell me there's an angel in your tree
Did he say he'd come to call on me
For things are getting desperate in our home
Living in the parish of the restless folks I know

Bring your family down to the riverside
Look to the east to see where the fat stock hide
Behind four walls of stone the rich man sleeps
It's time we put the flame torch to their keep

Burn down the mission
Burn it down to stay alive
It's our only chance of living
Take all you need to live inside[40]

Some argue for Utopian spirit, e.g.,

"Imagine"

(Lyrics by John Lennon)

Imagine no possessions
I wonder if you can
No need for greed or hunger a brotherhood of man
Imagine all the people
Sharing all the world...

You may say I'm a dreamer
But I'm not the only one
I hope someday you'll join us
And the world will be as one[41]

The teacher could ask students to write a list of critical questions they would like to ask the writer about the proposed solution. For example, with respect to John Lennon's "Imagine" students might list:

Hasn't the money from your work helped England?
How would "no possessions" eliminate hunger?
What if some people don't want to go along?
Would you take away all possessions—everything?
Would "no possessions" end greed?
How would possessions be taken away?
Can people be convinced to give up what they have?
Would you personally give up your millions to achieve the goal
  you have in mind?
Why should people work if they don't get anything for it?

Conclusion

It is virtually certain that this last question will emerge from any students who have studied economics since much of economic theory is based on the assumption that, in general, each individual will pursue his or her own self-interest.

> In mixed market economies perhaps the most important motivating force behind economic behavior is individual self-interest. Consumers allocate their limited incomes to increase their total satisfaction. Producers seek to maximize their profit and are pushed by the profit motive to combine productive resources in the most efficient ways to produce the goods and services consumers want to buy. Workers seek to sell their labor where the return in money and working conditions is highest, just as savers search out high interest rates in capital markets; both are motivated by self-interest.[42]

Notes

1. Robert B. Bangs, *Men, Money, and Markets: An Introduction to Economic Reasoning* (Pacific Grove, Calif: The Boxwood Press, 1972), p.4.
2. Paul Heyne and Thomas Johnson, *Toward Understanding Macro-Economics* (Chicago: Science Research Associates, 1976), p. 455.
3. Thomas J. Hailstones, *Basic Economics,* 5th ed. (Cincinnati: South-Western Publishing Co., 1976), p. iii.
4. Tiki Parker, *The World's Worst Bumper Stickers* (Los Angeles: Price/Stern/Sloan Publishers, 1978), pages unnumbered.

5. Stanley R. Greenfield, ed., *National Directory of Addresses and Telephone Numbers* (New York: Bantam Books, 1977), pp. C344-C346.

6. *The Columbus Dispatch* 107, no. 293 (19 April 1978): A-1.

7. Paul W. Barkley, *Economics: The Way We Choose* (New York: Harcourt Brace Jovanovich, 1977), p. 7.

8. Suzanne Wiggins Helburn, John G. Sperling, Robert G. Evans, and Elizabeth J. Lott, *Economics in Society: Concepts and Institutions* (Reading, Mass.: Addison-Wesley Publishing Co., 1974), pp. 274, 277.

9. Thomas J. Hailstones and Michael J. Brennan, *Economics: An Analysis of Principles and Policies*, 2d ed. (Cincinnati: South-Western Publishing Co., 1975), p. 4.

10. Heyne and Johnson, *Toward Understanding Macro-Economics*, p. 34.

11. Judith Viorst, *Alexander, Who Used to Be Rich Last Sunday* (New York: Atheneum, 1978), pages unnumbered.

12. Sharon Bell Mathis, *Sidewalk Story* (New York: Avon Books, 1973), p. 34.

13. Carol Ryrie Brink, *The Bad Times of Irma Baumlein* (New York: Collier Books, 1974), p. 58.

14. Evan Hunter, *Me and Mr. Stenner* (New York: Dell Publishing Co., 1978), p. 30.

15. Betty Miles, *Just the Beginning* (New York: Avon Books, 1978), p. 7.

16. Ann Head, *Mr. and Mrs. Bo Jo Jones* (New York: The New American Library, 1968), p. 37.

17. John E. Maher and S. Stowell Symmes, *Learning About Why We Must Choose* (New York: Franklin Watts, 1970), pp. 15, 18-19.

18. Jim Eggert, *What Is Economics?* (Los Altos, Calif.: William Kaufmann, 1977), p. 3.

19. W. Lee Hansen, G. L. Bach, James D. Calderwood, and Phillip Saunders, *Master Curriculum Guide in Economics for the Nation's Schools. Part I, A Framework for Teaching Economics: Basic Concepts* (New York: Joint Council on Economic Education, 1977), pp. 10-11.

20. John Burningham, *Would you rather...* (New York: Thomas Y. Crowell, 1978), pages unnumbered.

21. Glennette Turner, *Surprise for Mrs. Burns* (Chicago: Albert Whitman & Co., 1971), pages unnumbered.

22. Beverly Cleary, *Henry Huggins* (New York: William Morrow and Co., 1950), pp. 50, 51, 52.

23. Frank Bonham, *Hey Big Spender!* (New York: Dell Publishing Co., 1976), pp. 39, 40, 41, 42.

24. Irene Hunt, *No Promises in the Wind* (New York: Grosset & Dunlap, 1970), pp. 8-9, 23-24.

25. Bonnie Meszaros, *A Guide to Trade-offs* (Bloomington, Ind.: Agency for Instructional Television, 1978), p. 3.

26. Helburn, Sperling, Evans, and Lott, *Economics in Society*, p. 276.

27. Office of Economic Research, The New York Stock Exchange, *Reaching A Higher Standard of Living* (New York: The New York Stock Exchange, Inc., 1979), p. 1.

28. Richard B. McKenzie and Gordon Tullock, *The New World of Economics* (Homewood, Ill.: Richard D. Irwin, 1978), p. 7.

29. Peter Kennedy, *Macroeconomics* (Boston, Mass.: Allyn and Bacon, 1975), pp. 12-13.

30. Eggert, *What Is Economics?*, p. 12.

31. Hansen, Bach, Calderwood, and Saunders, *Master Curriculum Guide in Economics for the Nation's Schools*, Part 1, pp. 25-26.

32. Ibid., p. 2.

33. Holly Near, "Laid Off," *Holly Near—A Live Album* (Ukiah, Calif.: Redwood Records, 1974).

34. Stevie Wonder, "Village Ghetto Land," *Songs in the Key of Life* (Hollywood: Motown Record Corp., 1976).

35. Kennedy, *Macroeconomics*, p. 12.

36. Joni Mitchell, "Banquet," *For the Roses* (New York: Altantic Recording Corp., 1972).

37. Steely Dan, "Show Biz Kids," *Countdown to Ecstasy* (Los Angeles: ABC Records, 1973).

38. Hansen, Bach, Calderwood, and Saunders, *Master Curriculm Guide in Economics for the Nation's Schools*, Part 1, pp. 25-26.

39. Joni Mitchell, "Big Yellow Taxi," *Ladies of the Canyon* (New York: Warner Brothers Records, 1969).

40. Elton John, "Burn Down the Mission," *Tumbleweed Connection* (Universal City Records, 1970).

41. John Lennon, "Imagine," *Imagine* (Apple Records, 1971).
42. Hansen, Bach, Calderwood, and Saunders, *Master Curriculum Guide in Economics for the Nation's Schools,* Part 1, p. 13.

Index

Advantage
  absolute, 84
  comparative, 84
Advertising, 67
Agent, 67
Aggregate
  demand, 42, 46
  supply, 44
Articles of incorporation, 70
Assembling, 66
Assets, 111

Bach, G. L., 131, 147, 150
Balance of payments, 88
Balance of trade, 88
  favorable, 88
  unfavorable, 88
Bangs, Robert B., 123
Bank draft, 103
"Bank multiplier," 113
Bank
  bankers, 108, 114
  commercial, 11, 100
  national, 109
  state, 109
Barkley, Paul W., 126
Barter, 91
Base year, 57
Benefit principle, the, 76
Board of directors, 69, 100
Board of governors, 107, 114
Bonds, 71
Brennan, Michael, 126–27

Budget
  balanced, 46
  government deficit, 46
  government surplus, 46
  surplus, 80
Business, 60
  big, 14
  credit, 96
Buying, 66
  installment, 96

Calderwood, James D., 131, 147, 150
Capital, 3, 36, 37, 41
  consumption allowances, 41
  equity, 72
  goods, 2, 23, 38, 52, 87
  share, 101
  social overhead, 10
Certificates of deposit (CDs), 104
Charter
  state, 70
Check
  certified, 103
  traveler's, 103
Checking account, 102
Choices, economic, 131–37
Circular flow analysis, 34, 35
Collateral, 106
Collective wants, 75
Communication, 67
Competition, 8, 61
  imperfect, 61
  nonprice, 64
  pure, 61

Consume
  marginal propensity to, 39, 45
Consumer
  expenditures, 36
  financial company, 102
  goods, 2, 23
Consumer Price Index (CPI), 57
Cooperative, 68, 71, 101
  producers, 71
Corporation, 68, 69
  private, 70
  public, 70
Co-signer or co-maker, 106
Cost
  implied, 5
  method, the, 41
  real, 3
Credit, 93
  book, 73
  card, 96, 104
  consumer, 96
  government, 96
  line of, 104
  union, 11, 71, 101
Crime
  controlling, 15

Debt
  public, 97
  private, 97
Deficit
  financing, 77
  planned, 80
Deflation, 17, 118
Deflationary period, 46
Demand, 27, 31
  changes in, 30
  curve, 31
  deposits, 94, 102
  determinants of, 28
  elastic, 33
  individual schedule, 27, 28
  inelastic, 32
  schedule, 31
Depreciation, 41
Depression, 116
Differentiation, 62
  concept of, 64

Difficulties
  administrative, 11
Discount rate, 114
Discrimination, 12
Distribution
  functional, 55
Dividends, 70
  patronage, 71

Economic
  efficiency, 16
  freedom, 16
  goals, 15, 18
  good, 2
  growth, 17
  institution, 92
  justice, 17
  security, 18
  service, 2
  stability, 17, 41
  system, 34
  want, 2
Economics, 2, 18
  new, 79
Economies
  directed, 4
  free, 16
  market, 4, 16
  market-oriented, 16
  mixed, 7
  traditional, 4
Economizing, 2
Economy, 2
  overheated, 121
  sluggish, 121
Eggert, Jim, 131, 143
Employment
  full, 80
  multiplier, 41
Entrepreneur, 67
Entrepreneurial, 36
Evans, Robert G., 126
Exchange
  floating rates, 89
  medium of, 92
Expenditure method, the, 41
Export, 47
  net foreign, 47

Index

Federal, 117
   advisory council, 108
   open market committee, 108
   reserve bank (FED), 107, 111
   reserve system, 113, 115
Financial institution, 102
Financing, 67
Fiscal
   dividends, 80
   drag, 80
   policy, 78, 118
Float, 86
Foreign exchange market, 86
Fragmentation, 10

Gap closing, 79
Goals, economic, 143–50
Gold standard, 89
Good
   free, 2
Government
   big, 15
Gross National Product (GNP), 22, 24, 34, 36, 57, 120, 121
   actual, 80
   "constant" price, 58
   "current price," 58
   deflator, 58
   is a flow, 23
   potential, 80
   "real," 24, 29

Hailstones, Thomas J., 123–24, 126–27
Hansen, W. Lee., 131, 147, 150
Helburn, Suzanne Wiggins, 126
Heyne, Paul, 123, 127
Hoarding, 38

Imports, 47
Income, 7, 18
   multiplier, 41
   payments, 36
Indexing, 118
Industry
   infant, 87
Inflation, 13, 17, 49, 118
   administered pricing, 13

Inflation, *continued*
   cost-push, 13
   demand-pull, 13
Injection, 38
Insurance
   companies, 11, 73, 100
   term, 106
Interdependence, 141–43
Interest, 41
International
   dumping, 85
   monetary fund (IMF), 89
Investment, 23, 38, 52, 93
   corporation, 100, 101

"Jaw-boning," 117
Johnson, Thomas, 123, 127
Joint Council on Economic Education, 143–44
Joint-stock company, 69

Kennedy, Peter, 143

Labor, 3, 36, 37, 41
   big, 14
   division of, 6
Land, 3, 36, 37, 41
Law
   of demand, 28
   of increasing costs, 26
   of supply, 29
Leakage, 38
Liability, 111
   joint, 69
   limited, 70
   several, 69
   unlimited, 68
Living
   level of, 85, 94
Loan
   secured, 106
   sharks, 107
   unsecured, 106
Lott, Elizabeth L., 126

McKenzie, Rich, 143
Maher, John E., 131
Management, 37, 41

Manufacturer, 67
Marginal, 38
Margin requirements, 116
Market
  demand schedule, 27
  factor, 38
  mechanism, 27
  open operations, 115
  over the counter, 73
  system, the, 8
Marketing, 65
  channel, 67
Merchandising, 67
Meszaros, Bonnie, 138
Middlemen, 67
"M-M" system, 14
Model
  conceptual, 21
  descriptive, 21, 34, 35
  predictive, 21
Monetary
  twist, the, 81
Money
  instant, 99
  near, 99, 115
  paper currencies, 94
  token coins, 94
Monopolist, 14
Monopoly
  natural, 8
  partial, 64
  pure, 61, 62
Monopsonist, 14
"Moonlighting," 99
Moral suasion, 116, 117
Multiplier
  effect, 40, 90, 113

National
  income distribution, 55

OPEC (Oil Producing Export Countries), 14
Open account, 97
Opportunity, cost of, 3, 27
  collective decision making, 52
  saving, 52
  work, 51

Paper gold, 89
Partners
  silent, 69
Partnership, 68, 69
  limited, 69
Payee, 102
Personal
  distribution, 56
  economic analysis, 51
  selling, 66
Phillips Curve, 77
Policy
  easy money, 117
  monetary, 113
  public, 19
  tight money, 117
Pollution, 14
Population
  explosion, 12
Poverty, vicious circle of, 11
Premiums, 101
Price
  competition, 64
  elasticity, 32
  equilibrium, 30
  index, 118
  system, 27
Price-wage freeze, 118
Principle
  the ability to pay, 76
  of increasing costs, 26
Production, 25
  factors of, 3, 36
  factors of possibility, 29
  possibility curve, 25, 27
Productivity, 138
Profit, 5, 38, 41
  motivation, 8
Property
  private, 8
  public, 8
Proportional system, 76

Quantity
  demanded, 30, 38
  supplied, 30
  theory of money, 118

Rationing, 118
Recession, 116
Regressive system, 76
Rent, 41
Reserve
  excess, 111, 114
  required, 111
  required ratio, 114
  total, 111
Resource allocation, 3
Retailer, 67
Retained earnings, 41
Risk-taking, 67

Safe deposit boxes, 104
Saunders, Phillip, 131, 147, 150
Save, marginal propensity to, 39
Savings, 37
  account, 103
  and loan associations, 100
  and loan institutions, 11
Scarcity, concept of, 2, 26, 126–37
Sector
  government, 90
  international, 90
  private, 90
Securities, 72, 116
Security, National, 15
Self-sufficiency, national, 87
Society, problems of, 18
Sole proprietorship, 68
Special Drawing Rights (SDRs), 89
Specialization, 5, 138–41
Spending
  direct, 44
Sperling, John G., 126
Stability, 93
Stabilizers, built in, 78
Standardizing, 66
Stock
  common, 71
  exchange, 73, 116
  holders, 69, 100
  preferred, 71
  shares of, 69
Stopping payment, 102
Storing, 66

Supply, 27, 29
  changes in, 30
  determinants of, 29
Symmes, S. Stowell, 131

Tax
  business, 76
  direct business, 43
  direct personal, 43
  employment (payroll), 77
  excise, 77
  export-import, 76
  household, 76
  import-export, 77
  progressive system, 76
  sales, 77
Taxation, double, 68, 72
Tools
  qualitative, 116
  quantitative (of monetary
    policy), 116
Trade
  entrepot, 86
  free, 83
Transfer payment, 18, 44
Transporting, 67
Tullock, Gordon, 143
Two-tiered system, 89

Under employment, 13
Underwriter, 72
Unearned increment, 7
Unemployment, 12
  disguised, 13
Utility, 65
  form, 65
  place, 66
  possession, 66
  time, 66

Value
  added, 23
  standard of, 92
  store of, 92

Wage, 41
  -price freeze, 81
  -price guideposts, 80

Wealth, 7, 18
Wholesaler, 67

World Bank, 89